The following is a sample of the testimonials received on our various state editions:

. . . eminently readable. . . .

—Edwin J. Ricketts, Deputy
Commissioner of the Arizona
Department of Real Estate,
1991–1997

*Many Realtors® might put this down as too elementary, but I wish
all my clients would review the simple steps provided here, and they
could learn to be an effective part of the teamwork it takes to fulfill
their dreams. This book has the exact things most buyers and sellers
need to know, but are sometimes afraid to ask.*

—John Foltz, President,
Realty Executives

*This book is a wonderful road map for the ever-confusing world of
real estate. It's like having your own personal coach in a box.*

—Melissa Giovagnoli, Author, best-
selling book, *Networlding: Building
Relationships and Opportunities for
Success* and *How to Grow a Great
Business and Power Network*

*We found the right Realtor® to list our home and made an
additional $30,000 by using the tips in this book. And it sold in just
three days.*

—Damon Sims,
Property Manager

Get the Best Deal When Selling Your Home in Silicon Valley

Get the Best Deal When Selling Your Home in Silicon Valley

by Mary Pope-Handy
and
Ken Deshaies

Gabriel Publications

Published by:
Gabriel Publications
14340 Addison St. #101
Sherman Oaks, California 91423
(818) 906-2147 Voice
(818) 990-8631 Fax
www.GabrielBooks.com

Distributed by: Partners Book Distributors
Publisher: Rennie Gabriel
Editors: Davida Sims, Merav Tassa and Kate Shaffar
Typography: SDS Design, info@sds-design.com
Cover Design: Dale Schroeder, SDS Design

Manufactured in the United States of America.

For Jim,
Brian
and
Clair

Contents

Section I
Selling Your Home: The Basics

Section II
Buying Your Next Home

Appendices

Acknowledgments by Mary Pope-Handy

Few things in life are accomplished in a vacuum and without aid, and this book is no exception. My entire career, let alone this book, is a result of the never-ending support, advice, encouragement and belief in me from my husband, partner, and best friend, **Jim Handy**.

Our wonderful children, **Brian** and **Clair**, enthusiastically welcomed one more new project onto the already full family plate with my work and with this book, and they have supported my efforts to do a good job with both of these.

My extended family is one of the most remarkable group of people to ever grace the planet, from my parents, **John** and **Pat Pope**, brother and sister, **Stephen Pope** and **Barbara Pope** and their families, who all live too far away in Massacheusettes, grandparents, aunts, uncles and a sea of cousins to the family I was fortunate enough to join by marriage. There is a consistent striving to keep the right priorities and values and to work towards excellence in everything. Their encouragement with this book is much appreciated. If I can make this amazing group of people proud, I know I'll have done a good job.

Special mention must go to my mother, **Patricia Buckley Pope**, who was one of the first female Realtors® in Silicon Valley back in 1956. She was a big success, well loved by many and deeply missed. Pat could always see the possibilities in both people and homes, and in me she believed and saw someone who would do well in this business. She had always spoken of writing a book called, "We're in Escrow, Now What?" and for that reason especially, the idea of co-authoring a book seemed like a very good idea and I'm sure she'd have been thrilled with the project.

My mother was the first, but not the only Realtor® who got me started on this path and helped me in my ongoing formation as a Realtor®. Many, many Realtors® taught, coached, guided and encouraged me, and some simply served as an inspiration, including **Nancy McCormick, Kenn Callahan, Dave Tonna, Brian Crane, Kate Davey, Jane Miller** and **Bill Lister, Gary Collins, Lynn and Dave Walsh, Dorothy Billner**, and **Carol Burnett**.

Friends and colleagues in related businesses have likewise assisted me in countless ways: **Wendy Tomaro, Carron Findley, Duane Serrano, Marianne Hayes, Debi Merchain, Broderick Perkins** and **Fletch Sullivan** as well as **Dave Doeleman**, a coach with Real Estate Champions.

Thanks must be given to my wonderful clients and friends for their business, friendship and referrals. I hope this book will be a help to them, and to the nice folks in their lives who may need assistance with their real estate needs down the road. My gratitude goes particularly to **Anne Greene, Rosa Swenson, Peggy Brown** and **Denise Hanson**: ladies, you rock!

And finally, of course, I wish to acknowledge **Ken Deshaies** for his inspiration and foundational work, as well as **Rennie Gabriel** and **Davida Sims** for their guidance and dogged effort to keep me on track. My deepest thanks to you three!

Acknowledgments by Ken Deshaies

There are those without whom this book would not have been written and they deserve more than the recognition given here. Their faith in me, at times, exceeded my own.

My publisher, **Rennie Gabriel**, and I have formed a partnership of ideas that has done several things. My first book, "How to Make Your Realtor Get You the Best Deal", has been much more successful than either of us ever imagined. As a consequence, we have both been able to bring a semblance of understanding and self help to thousands of consumers across this great land. We have also enabled dozens of Realtors® to participate in getting out the message. In the process, we have become great friends and cohorts. Not everyone will agree with our methods, but then, we have not been seeking agreement. What we have done, I would hope, is to empower people on both sides of the real estate purchasing process along with the professionals who work with and represent them.

Davida Sims contributed so much to this manuscript, and her efforts are more than appreciated.

The hundreds of clients with whom my wife, **Mary**, and I have worked with through the years have provided the fodder and the inspiration for this book. So many of them have become good friends in the process that our family is huge in its abundance.

Patricia McDade, founder and inspirational leader of The Entrepreneurial Edge, provided the initial kick in the proverbial rear to get me to do that over which I'd procrastinated for so long.

"You don't end up in the grave. You end up in the hearts of the people you have touched."

Disclaimer

We've tried, we really have. We have attempted to ensure that everything said here is accurate and relevant. But laws change, circumstances vary and there is always the possibility for error. Using the guidance offered here, along with your selection of a competent real estate professional, you should feel confident in purchasing or selling real estate. If your situation is complicated by any of a myriad of factors—the property is a business, farm or ranch, or it has septic tank, well, soil or title problems—we recommend you consult with a REALTOR® who specializes in that area. Or, you may want to hire an attorney or other professional who can assist with the specifics involved.

About gender usage: In order to avoid numerous grammatical messes and to make the reading flow better, we have chosen to make this book as gender neutral as possible. We have used *they* and *their*, even for one person, instead of *he or she, his or her* and so on.

About the term *REALTOR®*: This is a registered trademark of the National Association of REALTORS® (NAR), and anyone who uses that term as part of their professional identity must be a member not only of the NAR, but also of their local and state associations. We always encourage both buyers and sellers to seek out the services of a REALTOR® when possible. However, even though we recommend the use of a REALTOR®, we know there are many small communities in the country where there are no Realtors®. Often throughout this book we refer to "agent," "licensee," "real estate salesperson," "broker" and so forth. We do this because anyone who holds a real estate sales license must abide by laws, which we will cover in Chapter 2. These laws apply to *all* real estate agents in the United States, not just REALTORS®. To make the text easier to read we may also show the registration

11

mark as Realtor®. Please see Chapter 2 for a more complete explanation of this designation.

Again, please consult with a professional in your state based on your situation. You can also reach the authors directly through the contact information provided at the beginning and end of the book. Also, feel free to contact the authors for a referral to a REALTOR® anywhere in the country.

Introduction by the Publisher

For many people, their home is the largest investment they will make in their lives. This book is designed to help you, as a homeowner, get the greatest return when you're ready to sell that asset. But right now your house is your home. It is where you shelter yourself from the outside world, where you raise children and bond with your mate or express your individuality. When it comes time to sell your house (and your home) your thinking has to shift from a personal statement of who you are, or your values, to an investment vehicle that will appeal to the greatest audience. It needs to appeal to the specific demographics of your potential buyer. Remember, the prospective buyer will be comparing your house and home to all the others on the market that fit their needs, wants and desires.

A small change or addition to your house can add thousands of dollars of profit to you, while spending money in the wrong way can actually cost you thousands more than you spent. You will see many examples in the following pages, but here is one example: You could spend thousands of dollars on very high quality carpeting throughout your house, but if you choose an unattractive color that won't appeal to most buyers, (like crimson for example) you will end up losing all the money you spent.

Unfortunately, many people think they can save thousands of dollars by selling a home themselves. The requirements of disclosure when selling a home are getting as complicated as brain surgery. I guess someone in need of brain surgery could save thousands of dollars by reading medical manuals and then attempting to perform the operation themselves, but it would just be silly. Selling a home "by owner" is just as silly. How can the experience of selling one or even a few homes match the experience of a professional who does it day in and day out?

A study conducted by the National Association of REALTORS® determined that people who sold their homes themselves received 21 percent less than comparable homes where the owner used the services of a REALTOR®. Another way of looking at this is to recognize that avoiding the services of an agent and saving about 6 percent—or less—on commissions cost 21 percent of the sales price that could have been received.

If you were a homebuyer you might be thinking that you're paying 21 percent more when you buy a home through a REALTOR® instead of going directly to an owner. But based on national figures, the initial sale price an owner sets is well above the appropriate market price of comparable homes. In most situations a buyer working directly with a seller, with no agent support, will not know if a home is under- or overpriced. They won't know what inspector to hire to evaluate the integrity of the structure and systems, nor might they understand the responsibilities and liabilities of the other party. In many cases they will not know what forms and wording will provide the best protection if something goes wrong. And there are a host of other items that provide safeguards to both the buyer and the seller that they might not know. This book will cover all of these issues, and more.

In this book Mary Pope-Handy has teamed up with Ken Deshaies to expose the secrets of how Realtors® are able to get more money for homesellers and sell homes faster than those who attempt to do it for themselves. The authors not only share their own experiences, but have interviewed leading Realtors® from around the country in order to gather the best ideas and practices out there. If you are not already a homeowner but looking to buy your first home, this book can also give you invaluable insights into how to find the right home, finance the purchase and save thousands of dollars in the process.

About the Authors

MARY POPE-HANDY has been a full-time, second generation REALTOR® since early 1993. She has an extensive real estate education including eight college level courses in real estate principals, real estate practice, finance, appraisal, real estate law and so on. Through her special training she has earned the designations and certifications of Previews Property Specialist (estate homes), Accredited Buyer's Representative (ABR), Seniors Real Estate Specialist (SRES), Accredited Staging® Professional (ASP™), Real Estate Cyberspace Specialist (RECS) and e-Pro certification (Certified Internet Real Estate Professional). She consistently ranks as a leader in the Silicon Valley market and has won many awards for production and service.

Because of her reputation as an honest and dedicated agent, most of Mary's business is a result of repeat and referral business. She serves all of Santa Clara County/Silicon Valley with an emphasis on Los Gatos, Saratoga, Almaden, Los Altos, and the neighboring West Valley communities including Cambrian Park, Blossom Valley, Campbell, and Willow Glen. She specializes in selling condos/PUD's, single-family homes and estate properties.

Mary finds that clients here in Silicon Valley are highly sophisticated and above all, need detailed information in order to make good choices in buying or selling. Therefore, she is dedicated to the highest level of professionalism, staying current on everything affecting buying and selling homes such as disclosure issues, market conditions and the ever changing contracts to make sure her clients get the best information and advice. She listens to her clients and is responsive and accessible. In addition, she uses cutting-edge technology to both stay in touch better and to give her clients better and faster information. Her hard work, dedication and high-tech approach compliment her soft and gentle manner. She does not use a high-pressure approach to sales because she is committed to treating her clients as she herself would want to be treated. Mary's clients refer her frequently, as they recognize the benefit of working with someone knowledgeable, experienced, dedicated and above all, someone who puts their best interests first.

An area native, Mary was raised in Santa Clara and Saratoga, graduating from Saratoga High School in 1977. Venturing out-of-state, Mary attended Gonzaga University in Spokane, spending her junior year of college in Florence, Italy and graduating with a BA in Religious Studies in 1981. After college, Mary earned an MA in Systematic Theology from the Graduate Theological Union/ Jesuit School of Theology at Berkeley and taught religion in Catholic high schools as well as doing other types of ministerial work for several years. In 1993, Mary changed careers to better provide for her family and followed her mother into real estate, a career she loves and for which her background offered some advantageous training. In her free time, Mary enjoys spending time with her husband Jim and their two children as well as her extended family members, walking in her Los Gatos neighborhood, reading theology, and traveling.

To Reach Mary Pope-Handy
(877)397-5391
Mary@PopeHandy.com
or
see page 150

KEN DESHAIES is a REALTOR® in Colorado. Ken is an Accredited Buyer Representative (ABR), Certified Residential Specialist (CRS), a Graduate of the REALTOR® Institute (GRI), one of the first 500 Realtors® in the country to become a Certified Internet Real Estate Professional (e-PRO500), a Real Estate Cyberspace Specialist (RECS) and an Allen F. Hainge CyberStar™ (an elite group of Realtors® who have proven that they generate a significant portion of their business through the use of current technology). He was named CyberStar of the Year for 2002, and elected President of the Summit Association of Realtors® in 2003. He served on the committee for the Colorado Association of REALTORS® that spearheaded the change in agency laws effective in 2003. For several years, Ken served as the chairperson of the Professional Standards Committee of the Summit Association of REALTORS®, the committee that oversees the ethical conduct of association members.

Ken is a broker/owner of Snow Home Properties in Summit County and works in partnership with his wife, Mary. He began his real estate career in Denver in 1992 and has worked in Summit County since 1994. Located an hour west of Denver, Summit County is home to four ski resorts and the highest freshwater sailing lake in the United States. While selling resort real estate is similar in many ways to selling in a metropolitan area, it does offer some unique problems. For example, since two out of three buyers are non-residents, properties must be marketed nationally. Use of the Internet and extensive use of photography are essential to a successful marketing plan.

Prior to real estate, Ken owned a private investigations firm for twelve years in Denver, employing and supervising as many as seven investigators and serving for a period as the President of the Professional Private Investigators Association of Colorado. In this work, he conducted numerous investigations into real estate transactions and fraud claims. Many of the stories in this book are based on Ken's experiences, both before and after he became a REALTOR®. During much of this time, he was also a member of the Win/Win Business Forum of Denver, and was its president for a year and a half.

To Reach Ken Deshaies
Ken@SnowHome.com
or see page 150

Section I

Selling Your Home:
The Basics

1. Going It Alone

We chose Mary to sell our house when we decided to leave California and move to Virginia. The week that the first open house was to take place, we flew to Virginia to search for our new home, knowing that things were in good hands with Mary. We were in Virginia only a few days when 9-11 happened, one of the planes hitting only miles away from where we were staying.

Distraught, and stuck in Virginia since all planes had been grounded, we relied on Mary to keep us abreast of our house sale. We worried that the market would fall apart, that no one would come to our open house, and that we would be stuck with two houses on opposite ends of the country!

Mary was incredible. She answered each call and e-mail immediately (and there were many!), kept us up-to-date on potential buyers, and calmed our fears. It was Mary's wonderful responsiveness that really helped us get through that very difficult time.

—Jan and Robin Maxwell

Many people who are considering selling their home are not sure how to begin the process. Do you try to sell your house yourself, or do you first enlist an agent? And if you do want to try to sell your house on your own, will word get out to that perfect buyer? The bottom line is that no matter which route you take to sell your home, you need to educate yourself as much as possible. In this area, where the economic stakes can be high, knowledge is power. By reading about the following two experiences, you will see what can sometimes happen in the sale of a home, and understand why it pays to become educated. Although the names have been changed, the following stories are real, and may help you decide whether selling your house yourself will really save you money.

First Story

Jack and Lorraine want to sell their home. Jack decides they should sell their home themselves; Lorraine reluctantly agrees. In the language of real estate, these people are referred to as FSBOs (For Sale by Owners). Jack believes their home is worth $500,000, and using a common 6 percent commission rate, he feels he can save $30,000 by selling the home himself.

Jack spends money on newspaper advertising and holds open houses every Sunday, and after six weeks a buyer is interested. Jack and Lorraine are offered $465,000, and decide to take it; it's only $5,000 less than they would have received if they had paid a Realtor®. After four weeks the buyer cannot get loan approval and the deal falls through. Jack wants to keep the buyer's deposit, but after the threat of a lawsuit he refunds it. Jack starts over again.

Ultimately, Jack sells the house for $455,000. After closing costs and expenses to market his house, but not counting time and aggravation, Jack nets $345,000 after paying off his $100,000 mortgage.

Unfortunately, the story doesn't end here. About a year later, Jack and Lorraine were sued by the buyer because it appeared the home was in a flood-control basin, and the required disclosure to the buyer had not been made. Had Jack paid the $30,000 commission to an agent, he ultimately could have saved himself from legal exposure, been protected in the failure of the first sale and marketed his house to a wider audience; he might even have sold it for the initial asking price of $500,000. So in the end, Jack lost much more than $30,000.

Second Story

Bill and Sara also want to sell their home. Sara convinces Bill that they should work with a Realtor® and they choose Linda Lister. After Linda does comparisons of similar property sales in the area, she determines the home value at $480,000. She then makes recommendations on how to clean the house, rearrange the furniture to make it look more spacious and otherwise spruce it up with paint, wallpaper and landscaping. After spending $5,000, Linda feels the home could sell for $500,000, and lists it at $499,000.

Linda handles the advertising, places the house in the Multiple Listing Service, markets the property to other Realtors® in her office and at other Realtor® meetings and holds several open houses.

At an open house for other brokers (also known as a brokers' open house) she is told of a serious buyer who would be a fit for Bill and Sara's house. She follows up and obtains an offer of $485,000. Bill and Sara are on vacation when the offer comes in and handle the paperwork by phone and fax; Linda takes care of the required legal disclosures and, after some back-and-forth negotiation, the home sells for $495,000.

Because of Linda's relationship with a mortgage lender, she is able to help the buyers obtain the loan they need, even though it could have been handled by the buyer's Realtor®. Also, because of her relationship with the escrow company she is able to get reductions in the fees Bill and Sara have to pay.

After commissions, closing costs and paying their $100,000 mortgage, Bill and Sara receive $360,300, with no aggravation or legal troubles.

As we said in the Introduction, a study conducted by the National Association of REALTORS® determined that people who sold their homes themselves received 21 percent less than comparable homes where the owner used the services of a Realtor®. Sellers who wanted to save paying an agent commission received less than they could have. Buyers have the peace of mind of knowing they purchased a home based on actual comparisons rather than the seller's greed factor, plus all of the other services the Realtor® has to offer. Involving a Realtor® is a win for both the buyer and the seller.

Although these stories are not a guaranteed representation of the realities of selling your own home, what they do illustrate is that you must be educated. And often it pays to rely on an expert's education and experience.

If you do decide that you are prepared for the task of selling your own home, here are some important suggestions:

(1) Take the time to educate yourself about the process of real estate transactions. Know how the process works from beginning to end, and what contractual and legal obligations you will be responsible for.

(2) Know what transactions must be performed by outside professionals, such as inspectors, title agents or attorneys.

(3) Pay to have your house professionally appraised so that you price it correctly.

(4) Have your home professionally inspected in advance so that you know what might need to be repaired. Take care of the items that you can afford to repair in advance.

(5) Establish a marketing budget and determine the best ways to spend it.

(6) Look for a preapproved rather than a prequalified buyer. There will be more on this distinction in the chapter regarding financing.

(7) As a personal safety measure, *never* show your house alone.

Selling your house is not impossible, but it takes diligence, patience, diplomacy and a willingness to set aside your own biases about your home so that other people's preferences can be understood and accommodated.

Knowing the Process

Before you decide to sell your own home, ask yourself these essential questions to ensure that you are knowledgeable about these important aspects of real estate sales:

✓ Do I know how to properly value my home?

✓ Do I have a marketing strategy to reach the greatest number of potential buyers?

✓ Am I familiar with California's legal requirements for purchase contracts and real estate transfers?

✓ Am I familiar with the two major contracts in use in our Silicon Valley area and the pluses and minuses of each one for my situation? (If an agent helps a buyer, they are unlikely to use a contract out of a self-help book, and that might be the only form with which you are familiar.)

✓ Do I know what expenses are customarily paid for by buyers and sellers in my county?

✓ Can I ensure that the buyer is financially able to purchase my home?

✓ Do I have the necessary contacts to handle the closing transactions?

✓ How are my negotiating skills?

✓ Am I prepared to carry back a note if an otherwise qualified buyer does not have the necessary down payment?

✓ Am I prepared to give up a partial commission to an agent representing a buyer – or a full commission to a transaction broker or facilitator?

The bottom line is that you must make sure that you are prepared to deal with this major transaction. You should have a plan in place and you should know who can help you with aspects that you can't do alone. Just as money doesn't grow on trees, houses don't sell on their own. If you are selling your house yourself, you must be prepared to make a substantial investment of time. If you are not sure how to handle this complicated sales transaction, using a professional may save you a great deal of unnecessary complications and may still net you more money at the end of the day. Then if you really are prepared, no matter whether you have help or not, you should be able to successfully sell your home.

2. Using a Real Estate Agent

From the very first instant I began searching for a real estate agent, Mary Pope-Handy shone through. At first it was the expedient way she got back to me, and every time we communicated, she left no questions unanswered and *never* left me waiting.

I was selling a home from quite a distance and there were a lot of stressful issues to deal with, as well as legitimate concerns and fears. She was on top of everything before I even had to ask, and I felt a sense of comfort from her from the beginning.

Her professional manner, together with her honesty and hard work, enabled me to get through the selling of my home with minimal amounts of stress, and I feel she guided every step in a manner that gave me confidence that I had chosen the right person.

—Steven A. Daggs

Areal estate agent and a Realtor® are not the same thing. Both may be experienced in the industry, but a Realtor® is a member of the National Association of REALTORS®, and follows a specific code of ethics. (You will find more information on this in the following section, "Credentials.") Anyone who passes their state's real estate licensing exam can become an agent. They may also be referred to as a licensee or real estate salesperson in other parts of the book. There are no cost differences between hiring an agent and a Realtor®.

Although there are some costs associated with enlisting an agent or Realtor®, there are also substantial benefits. For instance, not only do Realtors® have access to thousands of potential buyers that a homeowner may not be aware of, but they also have the knowledge to make sure that you are protected both financially and legally. Additionally, there is some element of risk involved in selling your home, besides the obvious economic one. Realtors® know important legal disclosure requirements. Agents are well aware of the fact that you are allowing complete strangers into your home, and therefore know what precautions you should take to protect both your family and your possessions. But these are just a few of the reasons why enlisting the help of a Realtor® is a good investment. A Realtor® can:

✓ Use extensive data and professional experience to assist in determining the best asking price for your home.

✓ Provide information about your home to thousands of potential buyers and their agents.

✓ Screen buyers and negotiate an offer and a purchase and sale agreement.

✓ Take on potential legal obligations and risks.

✓ Take you through every step of the process, all the way to closing and beyond. A good agent will be happy to assist you long after closing if need be.

What to Look For

Credentials

Picking an agent is a business decision that should be taken with the same deliberation as any other important financial decision. You will want an agent who specializes in your community, who is experienced and who you are confident will work hard for you. You've probably noticed that when we've used the term Realtor® in this book, it is capitalized and the registration mark is used. There is a reason for that. The term Realtor® is a trademark of the National Association of REALTORS® (NAR), and anyone who uses that term as part of their professional identity must be a member, not only of NAR but also of their state and local associations. Anyone who is not a member, but is legitimately working in the real estate profession, is still licensed by their state real estate commission and can be identified as an agent, a real estate salesperson, a real estate broker and so on.

When Realtor® is used, however, it means several things. NAR members have training available only to members. They have the benefit of local meetings and state and national conferences where they can network with other Realtors®. Many deals are actually made for buyers and sellers at those events.

There is a price to pay: Members subscribe to a code of ethics, which commits them to conduct their business with a sense of fair play. The public has some recourse when they feel they have been lied to, mistreated or cheated. They can file an ethics complaint with the local association requesting that a Realtor® be disciplined, or request arbitration if they feel they have actually been cheated out of money. The Grievance Committee and the Professional Standards Committee of the organization handle these complaints. A member is always bound to submit to the grievance process when a complaint is initiated by a buyer or seller.

Members have to pay dues, and the Multiple Listing Service (MLS) charges other fees to maintain a membership in good standing, but the bottom line is that they are in a position to provide much better service to you than nonmembers.

Those who do not have the Realtor® designation operate independently. They often do not do enough business to justify the costs involved in belonging to the NAR. While not always the case, many are retired from other professions or otherwise part-time in this profession, so they are not bound by a code of ethics that governs their professional actions, and in some areas they do not have the benefit of MLS access.

So for starters, get a Realtor®. You'll usually find the designation on their business card.

History

If you were taking in a roommate or boarder, you would screen that person to see if you were compatible. If you were renting out property, you would take a rental application and check out the renter's references and credit history. If you were going into business with or hiring someone, you would be smart to conduct a background check. It never hurts to know who you are working with. The same is true with a real estate agent.

As consumers, we have a terrible history of picking professionals—doctors, lawyers and, yes, real estate agents. We get a referral from a friend, attend the appointment, and that's usually as far as we go. If we end up dissatisfied later, it's our own fault for not taking responsibility for our own selection. We need to prescreen, ask questions, get a feel for how compatible we might be and determine how well that professional can meet our needs.

If you have a friend in the business, it can be difficult to select someone else, but it might be the most valuable decision you can make. We have known people who listed their homes with friends who specialized in commercial sales but had never sold a house. You need to ask some questions before starting with any real estate agent.

You want to make sure that they are the right person to represent you.

Get an Experienced Full-Time Agent or A Professional Team

Many consumers find it uncomfortable to ask an agent questions about their background, experience, and so on. In Silicon Valley, we have many former high-tech workers who have come into real estate sales (as well as lending, appraising, and inspecting). It is believed that at least one-quarter of all licensees in the U.S. have been licensed for less than five years (and Mary suspects that number is a low estimate for the Silicon Valley). So check and see if the agent you're talking with is really experienced by viewing the California Department of Real Estate's licensee lookup site: http://www2.dre.ca.gov/ PublicASP/ pplinfo.asp.

Most full-time agents work 40 to 60 hours a week or more. They are committed to their work and to their clients. A part-time agent is there to make a deal when it comes along, but either doesn't need the income a full-time career produces, or isn't making it yet, and may hold two or more jobs. Your Realtor® should be available and easy to get in contact with regardless of their hours.

Similarly, real estate teams usually have specialists handling different parts of the transaction, so you will almost always have someone available to provide seamless service. This can be especially beneficial if your Realtor® is on vacation or busy attending to other clients' needs.

Questions to ask:

✔ Do you work full time in real estate?

✔ How flexible is your schedule?

✔ How available are you to show properties on week-days, weekends, mornings, evenings?

Get an Agent Who Is Busy

Ask your potential agent how many sides they closed last year and the year before. A *side* is one side of the sale. When one Realtor® has a listing and another one brings in the buyer, each produces one side. An agent who has closed only four to eight sides in a year is not doing enough business to merit having yours. Either they need money, just got started or can't get enough business to survive and are on their way into another profession. An agent who has done eight or ten sides is not making a great deal of money but is surviving and probably growing, and believe it or not, they're far above the national average. Beware of the mega-agent with the mega teams (10 or more on staff). Unless they are extremely well managed you can fall between the cracks because so many people are employed on the mega-agent's behalf that no one is personally looking out for your single escrow.

An agent who is doing 20 or more sides a year is very busy—usually for a reason. They have attracted business, hopefully because they have served people well, although some Realtors® generate lots of business simply through smart advertising. It is, therefore, important to get a sense of how many transactions were results of referrals from past clients. Keep in mind that many good agents also have teams and assistants working for them. The top 1 percent of agents probably sells about four homes a month but they likely have an enormous team working for them. Clients working with these agents must be prepared to deal not only with the agent they hired, but with a 20-year old assistant as well.

Questions to ask:

✓ How many sides did you close last year?

✓ Is that usual for you?

✓ How many sides did you close the year before?

✓ Do you have an assistant or use an escrow coordinator?

✓ If you have a staff, how big is it?

✓ If I hire you, how often will I interact with you? Will I usually speak with you or with someone else on your team?

Now that you know how busy the agent is, ask how many of those sides were working with sellers and how many were representing buyers.

Questions to ask:

✓ What percent of your business comes from representing sellers?

✓ How much of your business comes from referrals?

✓ Can I speak with five of your most recent sellers?

Check out the Agent's Specialty

If you are selling a home, select an agent who specializes in residential sales. If you want to buy an apartment building or a business, select someone who specializes in commercial sales. There are numerous specialties in real estate, and your agent's specialty should be consistent with your goals. Note that in larger metropolitan areas, Realtors® also tend to specialize in price ranges or with types of buyers. An agent who primarily sells estate properties in the millions of dollars won't have the time for a $300,000 condo or even a $600,000 starter home.

Questions to ask:

✓ Do you have a specialty?

✓ What designations do you hold, and what do they mean?

✓ What are the price ranges of the homes you market?

✓ What area/region do you specialize in?

✓ Do you sell commercial and residential real estate? Do you also do property management? Do you also do loans? (Some of the worst agents we have "do everything" and are good at nothing!)

Make Sure the Agent Is Technologically Current

In today's world, it is vitally important to work with professionals who are computer literate and have a grasp on the new gadgets designed to improve service to their customers. What does that mean?

First, many states require Realtors® to use certain forms in real estate transactions. Silicon Valley is a high-tech mecca and agents here have adapted quickly to using these forms, which come in several varieties depending upon their board membership, region, or preferences. In the west valley communities of Los Gatos, Monte Sereno, Saratoga, Cupertino, Sunnyvale, Los Altos, Los Altos Hills and Palo Alto, the real estate board is SILVAR, the Silicon Valley Association of REALTORS®. The forms, Peninsula Regional Data Service (PRDS), are available on the Internet. The rest of the valley, (San Jose, Santa Clara, Milpitas, Campbell, and Alviso) is covered by the SCCAOR board, the Santa Clara County Association of REALTORS®. These areas tend to use forms provided by the California Association of REALTORS® via Win Forms.

It is important to realize that if you are selling or buying a home in our valley, either forms may be used. The purchase agreement, in particular, is quite different from one to the other, so it is important to be educated about the ramifications of using one over the other.

These forms are almost always available on computer programs, which presents the quickest, most accurate way to generate contracts or offers to purchase. Those who continue to write their contracts by hand or use a typewriter to fill in the blanks on standard forms as a matter of practice, as opposed to the exception, are living in the past, demonstrating an unwillingness to keep up with the times; they may not be capable of providing the best service. In all fairness, some agents meet their clients in non-office settings, and in these situations, it is simpler to use the hand-filled forms, but these instances should be the exception to the rule.

Other types of software allow Realtors® to track their customers' needs, access increasingly more sophisticated MLS systems and communicate by email. Many Realtors® are wirelessly connected to their email via laptop or cell phone too. Mary has found that having email "in the field" is a tremendous advantage in quick response time to clients. Digital cameras allow photos and virtual tours of your home complete with interior and exterior views. Since some consumers use older computers that cannot view virtual tours, it is very important to have photo galleries of homes for sale with multiple pictures.

If the real estate agent you are interviewing is not able to utilize a computer, beat a hasty retreat. Make sure when an agent says they're computerized, they don't just rely on an assistant or a shared secretary to do all the computer work for them. Your house should have as much Internet exposure as possible. Your wonderful home could be passed over while a competing house that is visible on the Internet is quickly snatched up.

Questions to ask:

✓ May I have your email address?

✓ What is the address of your website? Do you have more than one? What others do you link to? What sites link to yours? Where else do your listings appear?

✓ Will you take digital pictures of my home? How many pictures will appear in the MLS, or in other marketing materials? Will you create a virtual tour of my home?

✓ What other unique marketing do you offer? For example, Mary's website does an Audio Tour and also offers a Fax Flier On Demand for those who call in and hear the audio tour.

✓ Do you also do print advertising or postcards?

✓ Can you show me samples of your listings, flyers, ads, Internet presence and websites?

✓ What is your marketing plan?

✓ What other technology do you use in your business?

Training

Anyone worth their salt in any profession continues to update their knowledge about the work they do. Doctors, lawyers and mechanics face an ever-changing world when it comes to their professions and must take classes to continue to be of service to their customers. The same is true of Realtors®.

State laws require continuing education, but the requirements are usually minimal: three or four one-day classes every two or three years. Good Realtors® find the time to take much more training than that. There are a number of designations denoting certain continuing education landmarks, which are often signified on business cards as acronyms following the name. While some may be in areas not related to residential sales, all show a commitment on behalf of the Realtor® to keep their professional skills honed, and that's good. Do not work with someone who demonstrates no interest in continuing education. Look for some of the following designations on your prospective agent's business card:

ABR—Accredited Buyer Representative—requires additional training in agency issues and a thorough understanding of what it takes to represent buyers. While your Realtor® does not need this designation to represent buyers, it denotes their commitment to doing so. Graduates are members of the Real Estate Buyer Agency Council (REBAC) and receive continuing information to keep them informed of new buyer agency issues.

ALC—Accredited Land Counselor—similar to a CRS, this usually requires several years and several thousand dollars to achieve. It's the "graduate degree" of land sales.

ASP—Accredited Staging Professional—this designates an expert ability to prepare or "stage" a home for sale in order to meet the growing needs and expectations of today's real estate market.

CCIM—Certified Commercial Investment Member—this designates an expert in commercial property sales, like shopping centers and industrial, office and apartment buildings. It requires extensive continuing education and graduates are members of the Commercial Sales Council.

CRS—Certified Residential Specialist—requires completion of numerous two- to three-day classes held around the country. It takes the average Realtor® a few years to complete and usually costs $5,000 to $10,000 in tuition and travel costs. It provides significantly increased and detailed knowledge in residential issues and is the "graduate degree" of residential sales. Graduates are members of the Residential Sales Council (RSC) and receive continuing information in a variety of ways to keep them abreast of new issues in the area.

e-PRO—Certified Internet Real Estate Professional—this is the only certification program of its kind recognized nationwide and endorsed by the National Association of REALTORS®. Those searching for a Realtor® can have confidence that e-PRO graduates are savvy with all aspects of the Internet. They not only take Internet-empowered consumers seriously, they are also able to meet their online needs.

GRI—Graduate, REALTOR® Institute—represents approximately 90 hours of advanced education beyond the training that is required to be licensed. It is usually the first step to becoming more informed and professional.

RECS—Real Estate Cyberspace Society—this membership delineates proficiency in serving the public with recognized skills for utilizing CyberSpace marketing programs and for effectively adopting special technology and networking systems.

SRES—Senior Real Estate Specialist—this designates experts in the field of housing for senior citizens. Members have received special training, regular up-dates and are prepared to offer the options and information needed in making life changing decisions due to the unique lifestyle housing issues and needs of our maturing population. Members can offer senior citizens "senior discounts" when buying or selling among other services.

There are many other designations. If you see one you are not familiar with, ask about it. Most professionals are proud of their designations and happy to talk about them.

Attitude

We just cannot end this section without a discussion about attitude and disposition. We have mentioned that a good, winning attitude makes up for a lot, and it's true. We'd much rather work with a newly licensed agent who really wants to help than some old curmudgeon who has been in the profession for years, thinks they have all the answers and won't listen to anything new. There are a lot of worn-out real estate agents who have "seen it all" still occupying desk space in offices across the country.

Your initial interview with a prospective agent will tell you a lot about their approach to life. Work with an optimist, not a pessimist. Listen to their answers to your questions. Are they saying, "Your house is going to be hard to sell," or "It might be difficult to find the right buyer, but I know that the right exposure can get your house sold."

It isn't brain surgery to figure this out; look for a good, positive attitude as part of your evaluation process.

Agency–Liability

So that you can understand how representation works, it is important to discuss the concept of agency. It's easy to bandy about words like *seller's agency* and *real estate agency*, but the fact of the matter is that *agency* is a legal term. Its use confers a legal obligation and some legal liability.

Let's say, for example, your parents are going to be away on vacation for an extended period of time. While they are gone, they want someone to deposit their checks, pay their bills and carry on business for them as usual. What they want, in fact, is someone to keep their best interests in mind and to act accordingly. They ask you to represent them, to handle the paperwork in their absence. In order for you to legally perform those functions on their behalf, they would have to sign a document giving you power to act for them in those matters. This document is called a *power of attorney*, and it makes you their legal representative. The person giving the power is known as the *principal,* while the individual who has been given the power is known as the *agent.*

If you were to call your parents' banker in their absence and ask to transfer money from one account to another, the banker would refuse—unless you can prove you are the agent of your parents. In order to do that, you would have to provide their banker with a copy of the power of attorney.

It is also important to understand that a person empowered to be an agent may be in a better position to handle the principal's business than is the principal. The agent is either physically in a better location to handle business for the principal, or is more knowledgeable about the matters to be handled than the principal.

Vicarious Liability

An important aspect of agency to be familiar with is *vicarious liability*. Most people understand that a liability is a risk; it's an exposure. You take on the possibility of a liability when you hire or authorize a person to take actions on your behalf. You are still liable (pursuant to a specific power of attorney for the transaction at hand) for that individual's actions. Your child could damage the property of another, and you might be held responsible for reparations. That is *vicarious liability*. It is extending your risk through reliance on, or responsibility for, others.

In real estate transactions, every time you engage a real estate agent to represent you, you take on some vicarious liability if they act negligibly or unethically on your behalf within the scope of their authority. You rely on your agent to analyze a situation, make and give expert advice and make recommendations on your behalf that are in your best interest. You have also engaged that agent because you believe their knowledge in this area is greater than yours.

When you engage a Realtor® to represent you, it will behoove you to ensure your agent is experienced, knowledgeable, professional and willing and able to work for you. California state law requires real estate licensees who are acting as agents of sellers or buyers of property to advise the potential sellers or buyers with whom they work of the nature of their agency relationship, and the rights and obligations it creates.

Seller's Agency

When you list your home for sale, you employ a seller's agent to represent you in the transaction. A seller's agent has, without limitation, the following fiduciary duties to the seller: the utmost care, integrity, honesty, and loyalty in dealings with the client.

The obligations of a seller's agent are also subject to any specific provisions set forth in an agreement between the agent and the seller. In dealings with the buyer, a seller's agent should (a) diligently exercise reasonable skill and care in performance of the agent's duties; (b) deal honestly, fairly and in good faith; and (c) disclose all facts known to the agent materially affecting the value or desirability of the property, except as otherwise provided by law.

Buyer's Agency

If you are buying a home, you can work with an agent as a buyer's agent. A buyer agency relationship exists when the agent represents the buyer exclusively in the real estate transaction. The agent works on behalf of, and in the best interest of, the buyer. Although the seller still pays the agent representing the buyer, that agent does, in fact, represent the buyer and not the seller.

If you are a buyer and choose to work with a buyer's agent, you may be asked to sign a buyer agency agreement that must outline the duties to both parties, the duration of contract, any fees (what fees will be earned, who pays and when) and any other duties required by the parties.

A buyer's agent has, without limitation, the following fiduciary duties to the buyer: the utmost care, integrity, honesty, and loyalty in dealings with the client. The obligations of a buyer's agent are also subject to any specific provisions set forth in an agreement between the agent and the buyer.

In dealing with the seller, a buyer's agent should (a) exercise reasonable skill and care in performance of the agent's duties; (b) deal honestly, fairly and in good faith; and (c) disclose all the facts known to the agent materially affecting the buyer's ability and/or willingness to perform a contract to acquire a seller's property that are not inconsistent with the agent's fiduciary duties to the buyer.

While buyer's agency seems clear cut, and usually is, problems can sometimes arise. That's why we use forms, exercise disclosure, and put things in writing. For example, in Silicon Valley, an issue arose that involved the same agency representing multiple buyers who made offers on the same property. There was a case where a buyer became very angry that the same brokerage represented four out of 20 potential buyers for a property on which he was bidding, and filed a lawsuit. Of course, with multiple offers, we never know who has the other offer, but most buyers don't understand this. So, now, in order to make everything clear for our clients, we use a form.

Dual Agency

This is not a new term, but its use poses a hurdle many feel is impossible to overcome. Dual agency exists whenever the same real estate firm represents both the buyer and seller. It requires the broker to simultaneously be an agent and advocate for both the buyer and seller in the same transaction. Obviously, this can create conflicting allegiances. When an agent with one realty company represents a seller and an agent in another company represents a buyer, there's little conflict. When you sign a contract with a Realtor®, you are actually retaining the agent's entire company to represent you in your purchase or sale.

In theory, a dual agent owes both the buyer and seller the same fiduciary duties as if the agent represented each alone. These duties include loyalty, disclosure, confidentiality, reasonable care and diligence. By consenting to dual agency, the conflicting duties to buyer and seller are reconciled and instead the dual agent is required to act with fairness to each party. In addition, most of the other fiduciary obligations are affected because of the contrasting motivations of buyer and seller, who have agreed that the consensual dual agency will not favor the interests of one over those of another.

In a dual agency relationship, your agent cannot give undivided loyalty to either side. The agent must simply present the facts and information within their knowledge and insist the buyer and seller make their own decisions, without pressure from an agent.

There Are Advantages to Dual Agency

As much as we feel dual agency is harmful to consumers, it does have some advantages. If you are dealing with only one firm, and especially if there is only one individual agent involved, your lines of communication are shorter. For example, if you ask your agent a question that requires input from the other party, you are likely to get a faster answer, as there is one less firm in the chain of communication.

To protect yourself, discuss the firm's agency policy in your initial contact with them, and ask them to explain how and if they deal with dual agency. Of course, the agent you choose will also have to be experienced and competent in the rest of the skills needed to serve you, which we will address in other areas of this book.

Non-Agency

Some states have embraced an alternative to dual agency: non-agency. In a non-agency relationship, the firm has no fiduciary responsibilities to either party. This arrangement is unattractive to consumers for the obvious reason: There are very few circumstances in which you would hire a firm that has no responsibility to you, and possibly no liability if they damage you. We recommend you strongly consider your options as non-agency affords you the least amount of representation.

Non-Exclusive Agency

In California we have something called non-exclusive agency. In non-exclusive agency, an agent basically just takes the seller's listing, puts it in the MLS and waits for a buyer. The agent will not spend time marketing the home or giving the seller advice. This type of relationship is often used in the flat-fee, or fee-for service brokerages.

Disclosure

In the past, it was up to the seller to inquire about the types of relationships they could have with a broker and what each meant. Most states recognized that this was impractical. How could an unsophisticated consumer be knowledgeable in real estate agency when even most brokers were not? A majority of states eventually shifted the obligation of disclosure to the broker. Presently, the law requires an agent to inform their seller or buyer about the different agency relationships upon the first substantive contact.

You must be an educated consumer. When interviewing potential Realtors® to represent you as either a seller's or buyer's agent, if that Realtor® fails to discuss the various choices set forth above, you may wish to reconsider your decision to employ that individual. The agent may be unaware of the law, or is intentionally not informing you of your choices. In either case, they may be doing you a disservice.

Types of Listing Agreements

If you are seeking an agent to help you in the process of selling your home, there are several routes that you can take depending upon the kind of service that you want. Whether you just need minimal services or want exclusive representation by a real estate agent to sell your home, you will most likely sign some kind of listing agreement. Face it, real estate agents have access to buyers and can sell your home much more quickly by pooling all their resources than you can with just a "For Sale" sign on your front lawn. Below are some of your options when signing a listing agreement, ranging from the *exclusive right to sell* to a *one-time show*.

Exclusive Right to Sell

If you are looking for the best representation and the widest market through which to sell (remember, the more potential buyers who see your home, the more competitive your price can get), an exclusive right to sell agreement with an agent you trust is the best option you have. With this kind of agreement, you work with one listing agent who will market your home through every channel. They will place your home in the Multiple Listing Service (MLS), market your home to the public and to other agents representing buyers, and possibly hold open houses to find potential buyers.

With this kind of listing agreement, you will get the full array of services from your Realtor®, while your Realtor® is guaranteed a commission when your home sells regardless of who brings in the buyer. However, this does not mean that your agent will be the only agent involved in the transaction. While an agent can certainly bring in one of their own buyers, an agent's most powerful marketing tool is networking with a whole array of agents who are representing clients interested in buying your home. This kind of arrangement can get your house the most exposure and hopefully the most competitive price, and you'll end up with the best deal.

An exclusive right to sell agreement is the most common type of listing because of the services it provides and because the agent is guaranteed a commission when your house sells. Therefore, the agent will be appropriately compensated for the amount of time, money and expertise that goes into the sale of your home.

Open Listing

If you are selling your house on your own but are still willing to work with an agent to bring in a buyer, an open listing is what is most commonly used. In an open listing, a real estate agent representing a buyer has the ability to show your home to their client if it suits the client's needs. If their client buys the home, the agent earns a commission.

There is nothing exclusive about this type of agreement and a seller can offer such listings to any agent who is interested. The only reason that an agent would show your home is because they have a particular buyer in mind who's criteria is a convenient match for your home. Therefore, in an open listing, no agent will bother to market your home or place it in the MLS because they will only earn a commission through a buyer that they bring in.

One-Time Show

A one-time show listing is similar to an open listing. With a one-time show listing, the seller is not represented by an agent but allows an agent to bring in one of their buyers and receive a commission. If you are selling your home on your own, and an agent brings in one of their clients, they might ask you to sign a one-time show listing. In this case, the agent bringing in the buyer is guaranteed a commission should their buyer purchase your home.

Like an open listing, your home won't be marketed or placed on the MLS. You will simply have to wait until an agent has a buyer who is interested in your home.

Exclusive Agency Listing

An exclusive agency listing is similar to an exclusive right to sell except the agent listing your home is not guaranteed a commission. For this reason, there are very few agents who will sign this type of listing agreement and, in the end, both you and your agent can end up losing. In an exclusive agency listing, an agent is allowed to list and market your home and will get a commission if they sell your home through any real estate agent or company. However, the seller is also able to find their own buyer, and if they do, the agent does not get any commission despite the fact that they put work into marketing your home. For this reason, many agents who sign an exclusive agency listing will not market your home because they are not guaranteed a commission for time and money spent. Most likely, an agent will just place your home in the MLS and see what happens.

Commissions

Commissions in this country have historically been paid out of the proceeds of the sale, so it has been presumed that the seller actually pays those commissions; however, this is not entirely true. Some professionals believe that because it is the buyer who actually brings the money to the transaction, the buyer pays the commission.

In addition, any party to a transaction may pay any broker's compensation, without creating or terminating any agency relationship within that transaction. And more importantly, home values in this country are established with real estate commissions factored in, because home sales have been, and almost always are, handled by real estate agents. The cost of that handling becomes part of the ultimate sale price and value of the home. Therefore, it becomes a moot point who pays the commission—it is simply part of the home value, paid out of the proceeds of the sale. Please be aware that listing commission amounts or percentages are negotiable, and the form of commission agreed to may vary as well. There is no "standard" or "normal" commission.

One thing to be aware of is that agents are not allowed to charge you any fee on top of their commission unless it is explicitly stated in the contract. Hopefully you will select a professional Realtor® and therefore avoid these excess charges, but it is always important to know your rights before you enlist any personal representative.

It is increasingly common to see agents charge buyers or sellers a "transaction fee". This is used, most often, to pay for an in-house escrow coordinator (in essence, an assistant for the agent). Some commission agreements reveal what amount of the commission being charged will be offered to a cooperating broker. You should always know both what this amount is and also how this compares to homes for sale and selling in your neighborhood, as some agents may keep the lion's share of the commission for themselves and offer a fraction of what you are expecting to a cooperating broker.

The bottom line is that you should not let the dollar amount of a Realtor®'s commission scare you away. It can be negotiable and it can be an invaluable investment. Just as in many complex transactions, expertise costs money, but it is usually well worth the price. You usually get what you pay for, so get the best!

People tend to focus on what is predictable and measurable, like the commission. But a skilled agent can often work the market so much to the client's favor that they can benefit the client far more than the commission rate earned. Mary has sold homes in seller's markets where the seller thought she'd just stick a sign in the yard, put it in the MLS and get a good price. Instead, by going the extra mile, Mary got the clients far more than 10 percent over where it "should have sold". So yes, a minimal approach can sell a home in a crazy market, but going the extra mile can get a better sale price that, in the end, will more than pay for the total commission.

3. The Role of the Internet

Mollie Wasserman's Real Estate Internet Warning©

Despite advertising claims to the contrary, the Internet is *not* an experienced real estate professional. It cannot consult, counsel, advise, have knowledge of local laws and market conditions, make judgments, "own" the result or, most importantly, understand your individual goals and needs and care about you as a client. Furthermore, data by itself can be very misleading. To obtain an accurate interpretation of any information you're receiving online, please contact us.

—Mollie Wasserman

Given the revolution in technology that we've experienced over the last few years we must look at *what technology can and cannot do*. This differentiation is especially crucial when dealing with real estate, an environment where online companies clutter the bandwidth and your inbox with schemes to save incredible amounts of money and time by using their services.

Now let's be clear: Technology, and specifically the Internet, is a wonderful thing! Technology is a fabulous way to gather data and can do *functionary* tasks better, faster and cheaper than any human being ever could. But the danger does not lie in understanding that technology. The danger is that by itself, the Internet can never provide the *fiduciary* counsel required in services such as mortgage lending, law and real estate.

Functionary, fiduciary—why do we keep using these "f" words? Simply, it's very important to understand the difference between the data that you can get online and the advice, counsel and interpretation of that data that only your Realtor® can provide if you're to get the best deal when you sell a home.

Information Versus Knowledge

As Internet-savvy Realtors® who generate a significant portion of our business online, we are big believers in the free flow of information. You will find that both online and off, this new breed of Realtor® usually provides the most complete sources of information that you'll find anywhere.

Yet, we have had many of our colleagues question why we give out so much information, often saying: "If you give out too much information, people will have no reason to call you." We disagree. Although we give out information freely, we have never had a shortage of requests to retain our services. That's because there's a big difference between *information* and *knowledge*.

John Tuccillo states in his book *The Eight New Rules of Real Estate*, "Information is a collection of facts or observations about reality. Knowledge is actionable." In today's information age, consumers can increasingly get all the information that they want or need, but it's useless unless someone with expertise in the field can provide the knowledge to allow them to correctly act on it. *Information, without the context of a pro who can share the day-to-day knowledge of the industry, is just* data. *If a consumer were to act on it without context, they could very well reach incorrect conclusions and achieve undesirable results.*

Information is like sand on a beach—it's plentiful and anyone can find it. But if you want to build a sandcastle, you may want to consult the Sandmaster who lives on the beach, who can tell you how much water to use, what weather conditions are best for building, and most importantly, when the tide comes in and how far up. Without this knowledge, you could spend an entire afternoon building a great sandcastle, only to have it washed away!

Myths Involving Real Estate and the Internet

People love to surf the Internet when it comes to real estate. It's estimated that last year, between 70 and 80 percent of homebuyers started their search online. But there are definitely myths about what the Internet can and cannot do. The following myth is one of our favorites:

"The Internet is great! I can . . .

- buy a book

- buy an airline ticket

- buy or sell a house

- get legal advice

- receive a medical opinion

    . . . *all* online!"

At what point did the above statement step over the line from fact to myth? If you say after number two, the airline ticket, give yourself a gold star! What's the difference between the first two products and the last three services? Simple. *The first two are commodities bought mostly by price, the last three are services that require counsel, advice, knowledge and understanding of your individual needs.* The first two are functionary products, the last three are fiduciary services. You can purchase the first two products entirely online and probably save money in the process. In regards to the last three services, the Internet is a great place to start your search for service providers. But if you try to "go it alone" with just the data you find online, you will very likely risk losing your shirt if you don't consult a local provider who understands your individual needs and is accountable for their services.

Let's look at a couple of obvious examples before turning to real estate. Let's say there's an online site called WeKnowLaw.com. For $39.95, payable in advance by credit card, you can receive a "legal opinion." Does this opinion come from an attorney, a paralegal or a truck driver? The site *says* it's from an attorney, but how do you know for sure? And what if you take this legal advice and your case turns out badly? How do you get out of the deeper legal dilemma you're now in? Local attorneys who are dependent on referrals for future business have a great incentive to stand behind their advice and counsel. Does whoever at WeKnowLaw out there in Dot-Com Land care if you're unhappy with their opinion? In other words, what happens if something goes wrong?

Then there are the online mortgage companies that advertise everywhere. If you've read the business section of the paper lately, you know that many of these companies are not doing so well. Why is this? Well, there are a couple of reasons. First, much of the mortgage process still has to be done locally, so there's little economy to doing the process online, and more importantly, many consumers are finally catching on that interest rates and financing programs are very vulnerable to the old bait and switch that we mentioned earlier. Do you really think for a moment that the online mortgage company in Anywhere Land is particularly concerned if you're unhappy with their services? Local mortgage lenders derive business from local Realtors® and the community. Therefore, they have to make the situation right because they must be *accountable*! The national dot-com isn't. Now, as we said earlier, the Internet is a wonderful place to shop rates and programs and to educate yourself on the mortgage process. But afterwards, do yourself a favor and bring the best package to your Realtor's® recommended lender and ask if they can match it. Either they will, or they'll tell you why they can't.

Have you ever been to a medical website? There are many wonderful sites out there. If you were to go to one to become a more educated patient, and then take your questions and concerns to your doctor, that would be a very smart use of the Internet. If, however, you were to go to a site and attempt to diagnose yourself, that would be a very unintelligent use of information, with potentially disastrous results.

Real estate is an interesting field in that it combines functionary tasks with fiduciary counsel. Functionary tasks such as property searches or accessing home sales data can always be done cheaper, faster and better by technology. If that was the whole of real estate, we'd be the first to applaud the national dot-coms popping up online promising to provide you these services without your having to leave the computer. But the problem is, these companies don't tell you what you *don't* get. For example, there are a few companies that heavily advertise that you can get a *free* home valuation on line. All you have to do is give them a street address and it's yours. So what do you get? (Drum roll please.) It is possible that you might only receive a list of homes sold within a one-mile radius of that address. Some companies farm your information out to several agents, others to only one agent, and some might have automated responses that do not take into account any of the particulars of your neighborhood. But in all cases, unless your home has been on the market, none of them has seen the inside of your home, noted its pluses and minuses and exact location, and therefore, will not be terribly precise. Does this "home valuation," coming from a national site, take into account the power plant going in two blocks away from this home which will affect its value? Has it seen the inside of the home to find out how it compares with others? Does it take into account the railroad tracks on the next street? What about the local economy and the fact that young professionals are moving into the area, accelerating the increase in prices? What about sewer abatements or the newest regulations? A national dot-com can't advise you of any of those things, which could greatly affect the value of the property; but a Realtor® who's working in your interest can. Some of these sites will connect you with people who know your exact location and will be aware of the pluses and minuses of your particular street, but others won't! And even an expert who knows your street can only give you a range of 5-10 percent of the value of your home "sight unseen".

Please remember that while the Internet can provide information, it cannot interpret it! A Realtor®'s real value is not just in using technology to market your home, but bringing those buyers to you and helping you make the most money when selling your home!

4. How Much Is Your Home Really Worth?

Mary Pope-Handy's knowledge of the needs of her clients has enabled her to become a highly respected Realtor®. She helped me find a home that fit my needs in a very short period of time. It has been a pleasure working with her.

—Joyce Evans

When you are ready to sell your home, you must determine the "asking" price with your Realtor®'s advice. This may be a compromise between the fair market value and the price that you hope to get, depending on your market conditions and strategy. Once you determine this number, you should also adjust it to make sure that you leave room to negotiate with prospective buyers. Although this sounds like we are telling you to expect to negotiate down the sales price, you should know that in some markets you may get the opportunity to negotiate up! So unlike many other purchases in this country, real estate prices should always be negotiable.

Here is another reason to hire a Realtor®. A good, experienced Realtor® in your area will often know just by looking at your home and providing you with a market analysis, what it can expect to sell for in the current market. Not only might they know the sale prices of similar homes that have sold in the neighborhood, but your Realtor® may know the homes' original listing prices and how much sellers in your neighborhood have been willing to negotiate on price and terms.

Whether or not you decide to use a Realtor®, there are two predominant ways to determine a home's value: an appraisal and a comparative market analysis. What you should expect to learn through either process is the approximate value of your home. The reality is that until your home actually sells, there is no precise way to determine exactly what your home is worth. In the business, we say that your home is worth exactly what someone pays for it. An appraiser will tell you that a home's value is equal to an amount agreed to between an able and willing buyer and an able and willing seller, when neither person is unduly influenced by outside forces.

A word of caution here on pricing and choosing a Realtor®. It is important to choose a Realtor® because of their experience, referrals, marketing plan, and so on, and not because they tell you a price you want to hear, one that is far higher than what is reasonable! While most agents will do their very best to give you an honest valuation on your home in the current market, some may offer an inflated price in hopes of winning the listing, only to later insist on many price reductions until the home is within current range. This is called "buying the listing". If a home needs to be reduced several times before it sells, it will most likely sell for far less than it's really worth. So first pick your agent, then work together on a realistic price. Choosing the agent who tells you the number you want to hear, when that is simply not feasible, is not a plan that will benefit you in the long run. Honest real estate professionals will tell you that they have "lost listings" by telling the truth when the seller did not want to hear it. Pick an agent with integrity and you will both be successful!

Home Appraisal

Although an appraisal is usually ordered by the buyer's lender to satisfy lending requirements, it can also be a worthwhile investment for a seller. Appraisals are commonly seen as the best way to determine your home's most precise value. In California, a home appraisal should only be done by a licensed appraiser, and your Realtor® can usually provide a referral to a competent one. The appraiser reviews various factors to determine the approximate sale price of your home. These factors include looking at historical records of the property and the area, looking at the property's prior sales performance and reviewing the current condition of the property. For more detailed information on how appraisals work, contact the Appraisal Institute at 875 Michigan Ave. Suite 2400, Chicago, IL 60611, or www.appraisalinstitute.org.

There are also ways in which you as the homeowner can ensure that the appraisal looks out for your best interests. First, you should make sure that your house is in the best possible condition (see more on this in Chapter 6). You should also make sure that the appraiser is both licensed and qualified. Some states have few or no requirements regarding who can appraise homes; therefore, there are some appraisers who will incorrectly value your home due to inexperience. Don't be afraid to ask the appraiser how long they have been working in the profession and how many homes they have appraised in your area in the last few months.

Market Value

The most common method used by Realtors® to determine the sales price of your home is a comparative (or competitive) market analysis (CMA). A CMA is an estimated value of your home, based on the sales price and similar attributes of other properties in the area. CMA's may be less precise than appraisals, but they are generally a reliable method for determining the asking price of your home.

While less reliable than a local Realtor® who is familiar with your market, another source for obtaining a CMA is the Internet. There are now many on-line companies that will analyze sales information of residential properties, and for a nominal charge will value your home based on sales prices in your area. However, you should also be aware that online CMAs often only search public geographical records to determine a home's value, so they can not take into consideration the condition or precise location of a home. In the end, they can be very far off from the actual selling price, and will probably be within 5–10 percent of your home's sales price if your online CMA is done by a local agent. Although these services are not yet available in all areas, it certainly seems to be the new trend in roughly determining home values.

It will also help if, with your Realtor®, you look at other comparable homes currently on the market in your area and compare their similarities and differences. This will help you decide the list price of your home, and help you see exactly who you may be competing against for that perfect buyer.

We will generally recommend a range. A lot of agents would suggest that you can start in the high end of that range if you are not in a hurry to sell, and you are more interested in maximizing your profit, or net return. You would list in the low end of that range if your goal is to sell quickly. In Silicon Valley, as in most places in California, homes that sell fast tend to sell for the best price. If a home is on the market for a long time, it actually tends to sell for *less* than what it is worth! If your price is a little low, a competitive, housing-short market will likely adjust the price up. But if your price is significantly high, the home will stay on the market far too long and become a bargain down the road for a patient buyer.

Remember that regardless of what list price you choose, the actual sales price may be slightly higher or lower. But if for some reason your house is not selling, and it has been well staged, easily accessible, and well marketed, you and your Realtor® should consider lowering the price. Also keep in mind that even if you stage and price the home correctly, if you make the home difficult to be seen, it will not likely sell for the best price because you'll have cut traffic to the home significantly! Beware of having your mind set on some magic number given by a CMA. Remember that these are only approximations of the real value of your home. The economy, and the market, can actually change in relatively short periods of time. In addition, no matter how you try to determine a price, your home may have peculiarities that are just not present in any other home.

5. Selling Your Home in an Up or Down Market

We recently sold a home with Mary Pope-Handy. We learned from her how she approached real estate, her ethics, and the type of clients she prefers to work with. We would highly recommend Mary Pope-Handy to anyone looking for a competent, hard working agent (and who isn't?). We started the transaction as agent and client, and have ended up friends.

—Robert and Shirley Hausafus

Although the asking price may need slight modifications, regardless of the real estate market, a good Realtor® will be able to help you sell your home. This may be important to the many sellers out there who cannot wait for a market turnaround. The reality is, if the house is priced fairly and your house is in a condition that appeals to the average buyer and is given good exposure, you should be able to sell your home regardless of the market.

Besides the "asking" price, there are many things that can affect how quickly you sell your home, but we will start with price.

Price

For obvious reasons, the asking price is the most important factor in determining how fast your home sells. Despite the desire to make sure that you price your home high enough to make a profit, as well as leaving negotiating room, you should be aware that overpricing your home is the most common and dangerous mistake that you can make as a seller.

A home may be overpriced for many reasons. Some sellers consider their first asking price to be a "trial balloon," where they just want to see if they can attract a better-than-normal offer. Others simply insist that their home is worth more than any objective market analysis would indicate. For example, sellers who have been trying to sell their house themselves for months may now want to raise the price since they are paying a Realtor® for representation; the sellers still want their net price, so they try to add sales commissions to the listed price. Homes like this usually stay on the market the longest and end up being sold for less than market value. One of the primary reasons so many FSBOs fail is because the seller is personally biased. It is easy to convince yourself that something you own is worth more than its real value. It's also why so many Realtors®, when selling their home, actually list with other Realtors®, or at least rely on the advice of others. Objectivity is paramount.

Many sellers know of a home that sold for a high price in their neighborhood, and want to know why their home should not be similarly priced. But they may be unfamiliar with the particular differences between that house and their own that would justify the difference in value.

The bottom line is, don't overprice your home. Professionals know that the longer a house stays on the market, the lower the selling price will be in comparison to the original asking price. More often than not, your first offer will be your best. So if you overprice your home by 5 percent, you could end up losing 10 percent or more, and wait months to sell your home.

This leaves us with the question of how to modify the price of your home, in either an up or down market, to avoid overpricing. This is where a Realtor®'s advice can be invaluable. Unlike a typical seller, who is only familiar with the markets that effect either the sale or purchase of their own homes, an experienced Realtor® will have the knowledge of many years of market changes and fluctuations. They will also have a database of important sales statistics which they can use to expand their knowledge base. This can turn a guessing game into an educated pricing decision.

Depending on the circumstances, you may also want to consider underpricing your home. This option can be appealing when you need to sell fast, possibly because you are moving out of the area for work or to close on a replacement property. In the recent past, Mary has sold four properties where the buyer was the first and only party to see the property. These were cases where the buyers had difficulty finding the right property, the new listings were underpriced and they fit the buyer's needs perfectly. Even with full-priced offers, they got bargains. Good Realtors® check for new listings every day, and when a good deal comes up, they call the buyer immediately to see the property. Underpricing can sell homes *quickly*!

It is also important to know that there are buyers in every price range in your market just waiting for the next property listing. They've already seen everything that fits their criteria without finding the "right" home. If yours is priced right, and it fits, you could have a quick sale. However, if it is overpriced, the buyer may not see your home at all or won't make an offer. Overpricing can cause you to lose that buyer forever.

If for some reason your house has been on the market for longer than the normal range in your area, it's important to revisit the price, marketing plan, staging and traffic coming through your home. If you've hired an agent, this is a good reason for a meeting and a review of the above as well as of the feedback from showings. Some agents will say that the right price can fix any defect, and while that's true, it may not always be the cheapest remedy! Sometimes other changes will be as effective but ultimately cost less to your bottom line. What do we mean?

For example, if your home is not on the Multiple Listing Service, it's not being seen by most buyers and without the traffic you simply will not get the best price, if you get offers at all. If your property is only available by appointment and with 24 or 48 hours notice, you are probably discouraging showings and thus, limiting traffic and any potential offers. That's a huge mistake! If your home is overcrowded (clutter), or if there are odors (smoking, food, incense, pets), it is probably cheaper to change the environment than to lower your price. If you have hostile tenants or pets, these too can create an atmosphere that isn't conducive to buyers wanting to linger, let alone picture themselves living there. Vacant, completely empty homes can feel sterile and uninviting too. A little staging can go a long way in changing the way a house feels. If all these issues are addressed properly and your home still isn't selling, then the issue probably *is* price.

If you have had people looking at your home, but you still have not had any reasonable offers, you should find out what specifically is discouraging buyers. There are several ways to do so. First, your Realtor® should be getting feedback from both the buyers who saw your home and from the Realtors® who showed it. Not all Realtors® will respond, but the feedback can be invaluable.

A word of caution. It is easy to get defensive when buyer feedback indicates "the home is overpriced" or "the floor plan doesn't work." We have had sellers say, "Well, if they don't like the price, tell them to make an offer and we'll see what we can do." The fact is that most buyers, while willing to make an offer under the asking price, do not feel comfortable "lowballing" an offer. They simply feel that negotiation would be futile.

A good Realtor® will seek brute honesty in feedback and will convey that to you undiluted. And while an occasional buyer may respond too personally (e.g., "what a horrid floor plan"), it's important to look at all the feedback with your Realtor® to determine the next steps to take.

If your home has languished on the market for several months, it may be a good time to take another look at your competition. Your Realtor® can set showings for you on competing properties, and this could serve as a reliable reality check.

Negotiating Tools

In general terms, there are two primary approaches to negotiating a deal when price alone is the major consideration. One is to start low and know you will probably reach an agreed-upon price somewhere close to the asking price. In fact, one of the jobs of your Realtor® is to try to determine your bottom line. The second approach is to make a "take it or leave it" offer. If you only want to sell at the price that you and your Realtor® have determined is fair, then this is a realistic approach to take. Then buyers will only be able to negotiate on "cosmetic" items like the closing date or what is included in the sale. Believe it or not, we had a number of deals accepted on that basis, but usually when the house was listed for slightly under the market value.

The vast majority of real estate deals, when both sides are represented, should come down to what is fair. It should end up being a win/win situation, where everyone feels satisfied with the deal. We have all dealt with buyers who "want a deal" and who are unwilling to pay fair market value for any property. They want to steal it, to stick a knife in the seller's back and then twist it. They are only looking for someone who is vulnerable and has to sell at any price. We usually send away this kind of buyer.

Now, it is true some deals are made this way. We have found properties that must be sold quickly to avoid bankruptcy, or that are on the verge of foreclosure. We have not hesitated to get one of our buyers into such a deal. But your Realtor® is there to protect you from buyers who take the attitude that you can only be happy if you have "screwed" the seller. This attitude is really just corruptive of the whole process of real estate sales. This goes both ways too. There are always those on both sides of a transaction, buyers and sellers, who want to "screw" the other party. Again, the best deals that are made are the ones in which everyone ends up satisfied.

So, if you haven't already, you and your Realtor® should now prepare for negotiation by formulating a game plan. You should both be clear about what is vital to the deal and what you can give up. Most bottom lines should include some unnecessary items you can give up without feeling deprived, while giving the buyers the sense they won some concessions. It is also important to understand that there are many more things to negotiate besides price. In fact, there are occasions when price, although important in reeling a buyer in, is the *least* important negotiating objective.

For example, you may need a really quick close—you will lose a home you are trying to purchase and you need the sale proceeds immediately. If the buyers are renters, you may not have a problem; but if they also have a house they need to sell, it may mean convincing them to own two homes for a period of time, and you may have to concede to the offering price in order to get what you need. On the other hand, you may have just put in a brand-new lighting fixture that you would love to keep, but if it means getting your asking price, it may be worth parting with. In fact, we always recommend that you remove any items that you definitely want to keep before putting your house on the market, so that you don't have to say "no" and potentially waste negotiating power on trivial items. The bottom line is that it is important to know, and to clearly communicate to your agent, those things that are important to you and those that are not.

Always try to negotiate from a position of strength. You can contribute to a stronger negotiating position by not overpricing your home. It will also help if you have taken the steps described in the next chapter to do a lot of the preparation work before a buyer ever sees your home, from pre-sale inspections and having completed disclosures upfront, to staging and remedying any issues in your home so that it appeals to as wide an audience as possible. And, if you are looking to buy another home, it will be to your advantage to wait until you are under contract with a buyer before you make an offer of your own.

Your Realtor® will also try to find out what might motivate the buyers. While it is not always possible to determine their motivations up front, it is usually worth trying. For example, if you find out that the buyers are moving from out of state and need extra moving time, you can give them the time they need in exchange for taking the appliances. If you are not in a hurry to move, and you can make a closing date or possession date agreeable to the buyers, don't you think they might be willing to negotiate on price?

If you find out that the buyers are being transferred and need to move quickly, or are getting divorced, or are facing a termination of their rental lease, you will have accumulated information that is important to your negotiating process. Once you know as much as you can about the buyers' position, and you and your Realtor® have a clear picture of your negotiating position, you are one step closer to selling your home.

Another useful strategy to sell your home is giving the buyer a break. If negotiations are stalled, you might offer to throw in the patio furniture, or offer to clean the carpets after you have vacated. Small gestures can be very valuable. If a buyer is on the fence, a seller who appears willing to do something extra may have the right stuff to seal a deal. And at the end of the day, that $250 porch swing may have saved you an extra month's wait in selling your home.

Condition

You may not have control over the real estate market or your neighborhood's sales prices, but there is one area where you can personally make a huge impact: the condition of your home. Although this will be discussed in much more detail in the following chapter, making sure that your home is in the best possible condition will greatly enhance your odds of selling your home quickly and at a good price.

Ken works with a Realtor® known in the real estate industry as "Lox and Bagel." The nickname comes from the fact that he often "dresses" his listings for open houses, including setting the kitchen table with a lovely brunch including *synthetic* bagels topped with lox! Realtors® call this "staging" a home.

As silly as this sounds, his houses sell, and not just because of the synthetic food. On Sunday mornings, when most of his open houses are held, he provides his guests with an idea of what it would be like to wake up and have a beautiful brunch in this very home, which he hopes will soon be theirs. He even draws baths, complete with candles, champagne and strawberries. The bottom line is that when you view his homes, you know exactly how wonderful it could be to live there. Just as in magazine or television advertising, subtleties can make a huge difference.

It is important to realize that when a potential buyer views your home, you have your one and only chance to make the right impression. You may know that the dishes are usually washed and the lawn raked, but a potential homeowner only knows what they see on that first viewing. So before you cost yourself time and money, make sure your house is "dressed and ready" for sale!

6. Pre-Sale Preparation

As a homeowner and part-time real estate investor since 1964 I have occasionally needed the services of a real estate agent. I can state, without reservation, that Mary Pope-Handy is far and away the most thoughtful, informed, thorough and helpful agent I have worked with. If we could clone the perfect Realtor®, Mary would be our model. I recently reminded her that her initials M.P.H. also stand for Making People Happy. She has made *me* very happy time and time again.

—Karen Scarvie

Your pre-sale preparation is key to your success not just in selling your home, but in getting the best price with the least inconvenience. Most sellers will enlist the help of a real-estate-sales professional, and that is the best place to start. Find a good Realtor® early in the process and they will help you months in advance with decisions about inspections, repairs, staging, and so on. Take your time with this important task: interview, check references, do your homework, and then enlist their help in the preparation stage of selling your home.

Your Realtor® can help you make a list of needed improvements and repairs. Take care of the obvious things. Most buyers will want a termite clearance and other basic repairs made (leak free roof, no plumbing leaks and safe electrical conditions, for instance) and one of our local contracts demands it. There are many good reasons for a seller to do pre-sale inspections. One is that if the buyer goes into contract on a home knowing its condition, that buyer is far less likely to back out later.

When buyers do back out and a home sells again, it often sells for less than the amount it sold for the first time.

Another reason for pre-sale inspections is to avoid the experience of "writing a blank check" for repairs. One of our contracts requires that there are no leaks, that every system in the home is operational, that there are no pests and so on. If you sell and do not know the exact condition of your home, you may be promising repairs for which you don't even know the cost! To make sure you don't sell your home only to then find out how much you'll have to pay for repairs, do your inspections first. Not only will it keep you from "writing a blank check" later, it will improve your bottom line most of the time. For instance, if your bathroom floor has dry rot from water splashing out of the tub or shower area, you can do the repair and then sell a more attractive home that boasts a new floor. If you waited until a buyer was in contract to learn that the repair was needed, you would have sold at a lower price and then had the unpleasant surprise of seeing your bottom line shrink while the buyer enjoyed a new floor at your expense.

So hire qualified inspectors to do whatever inspections are needed to know what the basic condition of your home is. For single-family homes, this usually includes a pest and a property inspection at a minimum. If you're in a condo, it might simply be a property inspection. And if there are issues with various components of your property, you may need those inspected too: roofs, foundations, chimneys and pools for instance.

After selecting an agent and determining the condition of your property (fixing what you want and deciding to exclude other repairs or improvements once you do get an offer), you should be able to work with them to decide on a pricing strategy. The most common mistakes are made regarding pricing, and they are lethal mistakes to your bottom line! Know that you may have to revisit and refine the pricing strategy as you get close to going on the market. Remember that conditions such as the economy, competition or lack thereof, interest rates and so on can change.

Next you'll want to get the large stack of disclosures you must fill out, and begin the job of completing them. California is a very disclosure–heavy state due to a lot of litigation. Your best strategy is to disclose, disclose, disclose. And to make sure you do a thorough job, do it before a buyer is waiting and you're under a time crunch. Take your time and be thorough. Review it with your agent to make sure you are clear and have covered everything. Again, if a buyer can learn about the condition of the property before writing an offer, that buyer is far less likely to back out of the deal later. So make the condition known upfront!

Lastly, work with your agent on staging. We provide a lot of information on that later in the chapter because it is so important. Once your home is "dressed and ready for sale," your Realtor® can arrange the photography and videography of the house so that when it goes on the market you can hit the ground running!

Real Problems

There may be some real problems with your house that need to be repaired before you sell it. Except in a tight market, major "as-is" fixer-uppers are hard to sell. In fact, you should never spend money on cosmetic repairs unless you know that your home is structurally sound. If there are genuine problems with your home, you should either spend the money to address them, or understand that you will have to sell it as a fixer-upper for a reduced price.

A few years ago, one of Ken's clients, Tim, listed a rather old Queen Anne–style home that had been in his family for generations. He had recently inherited the home and wasn't particularly interested in fixing it up or living in it, so he decided to put it on the market. He informed his original Realtor®, whom we'll call Joe, that he didn't know much about the condition of the house, but that he did remember that the bathroom on the second floor had flooded a few years before, leaking through the roof and eventually damaging two of the downstairs bedrooms. Because the carpet had been replaced and the walls repainted, there was no visible sign of the incident.

Joe advised Tim not to say anything to avoid scaring away potential buyers. Taking Joe's advice, he accepted a full-price offer and never made any mention of the water damage.

During the inspection, the water damage was discovered and the buyers not only backed out, but they threatened both Tim and Joe with lawsuits for failing to disclose known damage to the property.

As it turned out, Tim came to Ken's office. He not only helped Tim with the mess that Joe had created, but he put his family home back on the market with full disclosure of the water damage, and listed it for only $10,000 less than the original asking price. Although it took a few months to sell, he finally sold the home to a handyman and his wife, because they knew that they could make the necessary repairs for under $3,000 and were happy to have saved some money! There is always a buyer for every home; the important thing is finding the *right* buyer.

A visual inspection will help you pinpoint potentially serious issues so that you can have them assessed by a specialist. You should also be aware that once you know about defects, you are legally obligated to disclose them to potential buyers. You and your agent must disclose any *known* material defects in your property. Although if you are selling your house "as is" and the buyer accepts any conditions as part of the sale, they still must be fully disclosed.

Dressed and Ready for Sale

Buying a home can be one of the most emotional purchases a person or family makes. A buyer may see that perfect bay window with the window seat they've always dreamed of and know that your home has to be theirs. So in order to have the most successful experience in selling your home, you must appeal to the *emotions* of potential buyers.

The reality is that what your home looks like matters, a lot! Deep down most buyers want a perfect new house, regardless of what they can really afford. No matter the age of your house, your job is to make it appear as new as possible without wasting money. Obviously, if your house was perfect you probably wouldn't want to move, but the point is to make it as appealing as possible.

We always recommend to our sellers that a good place to start is with a thorough inspection. Take a pad and paper and walk from room to room, writing down what you see. Don't just focus on problem areas, look for what you should highlight. Are there wonderful French doors hidden by worn curtains? Is the fireplace blocked from view by too much old furniture? You should not only tour every room, but inspect the entire property. Look at the house as if you were going to make an offer. What would you want to see? Maybe even enlist the help of an honest and impartial friend or family member to help you be more objective. If a buyer has a choice between two comparable properties that are similarly priced, they will choose the one in the best condition.

Dos and Don'ts

There are some very simple and inexpensive things that you can do, or that you should avoid, when you are selling your home. By following these 10 simple tips, you can not only increase the sale price of your home, but hopefully ensure a quick sale.

Remember you have a very valuable item to sell. So like a sophisticated salesperson, you should make sure that the product you are offering is useful and appealing.

Tip 1: A little-known secret of the trade is to make sure that you don't leave your car in the driveway. When a buyer pulls up they should see the home, not your cars. Let them feel like the driveway is theirs, and maybe even visualize themselves coming home. If you can't park your car in the garage because of clutter, read Tip 2.

Tip 2: Get rid of any and all clutter. Piles of books and magazines, snow-globe collections and bags of recycling can be such a negative distraction that potential buyers might walk right out before passing the entry hall. The goal is to make your house spotless. The less clutter there is, the more open and spacious your home will appear. Too much furniture and knick-knacks always make a room look smaller than it is. And don't forget the closets and the garage. Storage space is an important concern of many buyers, so the less cluttered these spaces are, the more space buyers think they are getting. Don't wait until you pack to throw out those unneeded items— now is the time to do it. These things cost nothing more than time, but in the scope of a sale can be invaluable. There's no need to make major changes, as most homeowners want to decorate themselves. You want to give buyers a spacious and clean blank canvas. If you can't part with these items forever, at least put them in storage for now. There are companies that will bring you storage units, you then load them with possessions that are not needed in the near future, and the storage company picks them up and takes them away. Once you have moved, the unit is returned to you at your new home!

Tip 3: If you have furniture in less than the best condition, it may be worthwhile to remove it (either by storing or donating it) before showing your home. Unattractive furnishings can distract potential buyers. It is usually better to have more open space than to fill it with marginal items.

Tip 4: You should avoid potentially offensive items. We usually preview houses before they show, or at least ask home sellers to have a neutral person walk through their home to see if they have any items that might be thought offensive to some potential buyers.

Tip 5: Avoid air fresheners. To prospective buyers, air fresheners seem like cover ups. You are better off making sure that your home has been well aired out, particularly if you are a smoker. In fact, if you are a smoker and have smoked inside regularly, you will probably do best to replace your carpeting, launder or replace your curtains and only smoke outside until after you have moved. Also, avoid using incense or heavy cooking smells; these odors, like smoke, could cost you 5-10 percent of the value of your home in a reduced purchase price! Likewise, indoor animals can tremendously hurt the salability of a home if there are lingering odors. This is especially true with cats, older dogs, bunnies, rodents and so on. Our pets are very much a part of our families but be aware that some buyers are allergic and many are concerned about the odor not leaving when you do. Try using strategic fresh flowers to add a touch of ambience as well as a fresh scent, or bake fresh cookies or bread.

Tip 6: Make sure that your home is as inviting as possible. This means turning off the television and any other distracting electronic devices. Instead, try using soft music to set the tone. You also want inviting lighting. Make sure you have high-watt bulbs in dark rooms and soft lighting in areas where you want to detract attention.

Tip 7: Another important suggestion is to make sure that pets and children are not around when your house is being shown to prospective buyers. It is best to assume that buyers don't have pets or children and let them ask questions about how a home can accommodate their needs if necessary. The bottom line is that if a buyer is allergic to cats or dogs, your beloved pet may drive them out before giving your home a chance.

Tip 8: If you have wood floors in good condition you should be sure to show them off. Conversely, cover any old or worn floors with clean and tidy rugs (but be sure to disclose that the floors are worn or stained in your disclosure forms!) Additionally, if you have carpeting, make sure that you have it properly cleaned. In fact, stained or dirty carpet is such a huge turnoff to buyers, that depending on the condition, it may be worthwhile to replace it with inexpensive neutral carpeting, or to just pull it up if it covers hard wood flooring.

Tip 9: You should also make sure that any important papers, prescription drugs and valuables are put away in a safe place. The reality is that buyers are strangers that you are letting into your home. Although a Realtor® will always be there to show your home, it is best not to take chances with your private and valuable items. It is not unheard of for drug addicts to occasionally visit open houses just to steal prescription drugs for resale or personal use. Toddlers left to their own devices may also momentarily grab something without their parent's knowledge. It's best to keep money, jewelry, medicines and all valuables out of sight.

Tip 10: Connected to Tip 9 is the rule that you should always have an agent present when you are showing your home. This is not only a safety issue, but how else can you ensure that prospective buyers have all the information they need to make an offer on your home? Buyers are savvy; they expect their questions to be answered by a knowledgeable representative. If a buyer shows up on your doorstep, refer them to your agent but do not let them in if they don't have an agent who has called ahead of time and accompanies them. In addition, the agent should always give you a business card.

Making the Buyer Comfortable

Potential buyers may be entering their future home, and can't help but emotionally connect with the surroundings. You can take advantage of this. You can make coffee or bake cookies. This is not only a kind gesture, but adds pleasing, comfortable aromas.

Another useful tool is to give a list of your favorite features to your agent. This way your Realtor® can draw buyers to the best parts of your home. What made you want to buy your home is likely a selling point for prospective buyers. The more your Realtor® points out to potential buyers, the more comfortable they will feel, and the less time they will need to spend learning about the home for themselves.

One area over which you may have little control is your neighborhood. Regardless, we all know how important a factor this is in buying a home. But don't fret; there are some small things that you can do that can make a big difference. You can help clean up graffiti in the neighborhood; you can clean up garbage in the street; you can have the city tow away inoperative or abandoned cars. In the larger scheme, you can team up with neighbors to form a neighborhood cleanup group or a Neighborhood Watch program. Prospective buyers may be relieved to know that even though you are leaving, they are moving into a neighborhood that cares.

Another thing that most buyers are looking for is a relatively modern home. As we discussed earlier, buyers want a home to appear new. Things that substantially date your house, like popcorn ceilings, metal banisters and wood paneling, can make a sale more difficult. It's worthwhile to look into the cost of replacing, painting or removing these items. It may very well be a great investment.

Today's homebuyer is looking for "character." Just as popcorn ceilings are out, molding and natural woods are in. Adding molding can be a relatively inexpensive do-it-yourself project with substantial returns.

If you are going to spend money on your home, aside from fresh paint and clean or possibly new carpeting, there are two places where your investment will have the greatest payback: the kitchen and the bathroom. Replacing kitchen counters and floors alone can brighten up a dated kitchen. Likewise, bathroom remodels can be moderately priced and can substantially update your home. You don't need to take any of these steps to sell your home, but be aware of what buyers will be looking for, and how you can best meet their needs. Just making your home sparkling clean can make a huge difference. Sellers must consider these factors and decide for themselves how much time and money they can invest in the final sale price of their home.

Exterior

First impressions are important, and the first thing that prospective buyers will see is the outside of your home. The exterior not only speaks for itself, but it tells potential buyers what they can expect to find inside. The reality is that if the exterior of your home is in a bad state, many buyers will just keep on driving. If you drove up to a house with peeling paint, dead plants and falling rain gutters, you wouldn't expect the inside to be taken care of, would you? For some small things you can do to make sure that the outside of your home is as well-dressed as the inside, see our checklist at the end of the chapter.

Amenities

The most common problem we see after a closing is that the seller takes an item from the property that the buyer assumed was part of the sale. This goes back to an important point that we discussed earlier: Make sure that items you want to keep are removed from the house before you show it to prospective buyers. The bottom line is that there are some items that will automatically become part of the property once title is passed to the buyer, regardless of whether you assumed it was yours to keep. This is referred to as the *law of fixtures.*

The law of fixtures basically says that fixtures are part of the property and cannot be removed. Fixtures are anything that is permanently attached to the property by attachments such as bolts or screws. Some items are easy to understand as fixtures, such as counters, sinks, or flooring. But some areas are more complicated. For example, a built-in dishwasher is a fixture, since it can't just be unplugged and removed, while a refrigerator is not, if you can simply unplug and remove it. Similarly, window treatments are only considered fixtures if they are screwed or bolted in.

Another common area of confusion is lighting. If light fixtures are bolted to the wall or ceiling, they are part of the sale, even including expensive chandeliers and antiques. The only way to avoid this problem is by removing these items (and replacing them with inexpensive fixtures) before showing your home. This is much more serious than removing items that a buyer may dislike, because if you show them, they become part of the transaction. Unlike nonfixtures (refrigerators, washers and dryers), a buyer does not even have to request these items in the contract.

If your home has a dated refrigerator and you plan to buy a new one for your next home, it may be worthwhile to buy it before you show your home. This runs slightly counter to the rule that you shouldn't show items that you intend to keep, but here there is a good reason. Think of your kitchen as a showroom. Unlike lighting fixtures, buyers generally know that these appliances are not necessarily included in the sale. Nice appliances can show prospective buyers how contemporary and updated your kitchen can look. Dated appliances really make a kitchen look old. Even if your buyers insist on keeping the appliances, if you make sure that you are compensated, it may still ensure a quicker sale at a better overall price.

Checklist

Begin with the Exterior

1. Keep the lawn mowed. A well-manicured lawn, neatly trimmed shrubs and cleanly swept sidewalks create a good first impression.

2. Be sure to fertilize your grass to make it look lush and green.

3. Trim or cut back overgrown shrubs. Doors and windows should be firmly visible and not obstructed in the least.

4. Paint the house if necessary. (If you do decide to paint your house, drive through new neighborhoods and choose a contemporary, neutral color. Don't paint your house the same old color it was in 1970.)

5. Clean stains and oil from sidewalks and driveways. A badly stained driveway suggests that the house may not have been well maintained.

6. Replace cracked or broken windows and torn screens.

7. Hose down the entrance of your house to get rid of annoying cobwebs and dead bugs.

8. Make sure the entry light and doorbell are in good working order.

9. Inspect the roof and gutters. Make repairs and paint as necessary.

10. Repaint the front door. A new coat of paint suggests a well-cared-for home.

11. Put a fresh coat of paint on your mailbox.

12. Be sure driveways and sidewalks are free of ice and snow (if you live in the Santa Cruz Mountains) in the winter.

13. Place bright, fresh flowers by the front door or along the walk. Have a new or fresh-looking doormat in a solid color at your front door.

Now Let's Look at the Interior

1. Begin with a full housecleaning from top to bottom. Clean out closets and throw away unused items. Make sure that clothes are hung neatly and shoes are tidily arranged. Eliminating clutter makes your home look more spacious.

2. Make sure the walls are clean and free of smudges and fingerprints. Give them a fresh coat of paint if washing doesn't do the trick. If your colors are very bold and dark, repaint to something lighter and more neutral. Dark reds and purples, for instance, tend to make rooms look smaller than they are and they can be overwhelming to many buyers.

3. Arrange furniture to make your rooms appear more spacious. Get rid of badly worn furniture or place it in storage.

4. Wash the windows, inside and out! Include the tracks! Make sure the curtains clear the window entirely when open to allow the maximum amount of light in.

5. Wash or replace the curtains or blinds.

6. If the carpets are badly worn or soiled, replace them with new carpeting in a neutral color.

7. Repair any sticking doors.

8. Fix leaky faucets and clean the water stains from the sinks, toilets and shower doors.

9. Replace burned-out light bulbs and make sure that all light fixtures are in good working order.

10. The kitchen is the most important room in your house. Make it bright and inviting. Wash the walls and cabinets or give them a new coat of paint if necessary. Clean the vent hood and make all the appliances gleaming. If the floor is badly worn, consider replacing it.

11. Make the bathrooms sparkle! Repair old caulk in showers and tubs. Place fresh towels and soaps in the bathrooms and add flowers or a candle (not burning) if there is room.

12. Clean the bedrooms and replace faded curtains and bedspreads.

13. Clean the basement, if you are among the few to be lucky enough to have one, and the garage. Get rid of items you no longer use or put them in storage. Make sure there is plenty of light, even in these rooms.

14. Make sure your house smells fresh and clean. Nothing is a bigger turnoff to a buyer than cigarette smoke, cooking odors, incense, a smelly dog bed or dirty litter box.

15. If there is a fireplace, have the chimney cleaned. Soot has an odor!

7. Screening Prospective Buyers

Mary knows the real estate business. She excels at every aspect of a home sale: property preparation, staging, seller protection, advertising, closing and getting the best price. She is conscientious and works very hard to get the job done efficiently. I give her my highest recommendation.

—Rob C.

Motivation

The motivation for selling your home will be a substantial factor in determining the kind of buyer you are looking for. For example, if you need to sell your home because you have been offered a job in a new state, you may be willing to look for a broader range of buyers than if you are merely selling in order to buy a bigger home. Likewise, a buyer looking for an investment property may want different things than one who is looking for a home for their family. Knowing both your motivation and the motivation of your prospective buyers can help the negotiating process. There are many types of buyers with many different financial backgrounds, and often a buyer with a 10 percent down payment can be just as good as an all-cash buyer. In fact, due to our astronomical prices in Silicon Valley, we are seeing fewer and fewer 20 percent down loans.

Conventional Financing

When selling your home, you will likely be familiar with some of the basics of financing based upon your own experiences as a buyer. However, there are some important aspects of financing about which you should be knowledgeable to ensure that your perfect buyer can actually afford your home. How the buyer intends to pay for your home, and whether or not they are qualified for financing, is really the most important aspect of the entire sales transaction. We all know that without the money, there is no sale.

There are three primary sources for financing the purchase of a home: banks and credit unions, mortgage bankers and mortgage brokers. Most people are aware that banks and credit unions loan money for home purchases, including the former Savings and Loan associations. Savings and Loans, banks and credit unions lend money directly to the buyer from their own pool of funds, usually based on customer deposits. The individuals that work for the bank are usually called *loan officers*. Loan officers are often paid commission in addition to their salary, which provides their incentive to get loan applications.

Mortgage bankers are also direct lenders and use their own funds, or those of wealthy investors, but they usually do not keep the loan. They will often sell off the loan to a government-sanctioned major home lender like Freddie Mac or Fannie Mae. You might not even know if your loan is sold off, as mortgage bankers often continue to service a loan by mailing statements and collecting payments.

Mortgage brokers shop around for buyers of loans, searching for the lender with the program or interest rate that fits their client's situation. They take the application and can apply to dozens of lenders like banks and mortgage bankers, and act as intermediaries between borrowers and lenders. They can't control interest rates or terms and are usually paid by both the buyer and the lender through closing fees or points. The points paid to buy the loan are often the same as going directly through the lender. One point equals 1 percent of the loan amount. Regardless of whether a buyer uses a broker or a banker, the key is making sure that your buyer has obtained financing prior to making an offer on your home.

Prequalification and Preapproval

The terms prequalification and preapproval are often used by buyers and their agents, and it is extremely important that you know the significant difference between them. The difference is like *thinking* you can afford to buy a home as opposed to having the bank say you qualify. A prequalification letter says the buyer earns enough money to buy a home in a certain price range. Unfortunately, this is based on information given to a bank or mortgage broker by the buyer over the phone. The lender may not have verified the buyer's income or run a credit report. Therefore they do not know if the buyer's credit is wonderful or terrible, or if they can secure a loan to fit the buyer's budget.

On the other hand, if a buyer has a preapproval letter, the lender has checked the buyer's credit, gotten basic information on their income and debts and knows approximately the size of mortgage the buyer will qualify for. Based on the verification, the buyer would be approved for a loan. Obviously, you want to make sure that the buyer is not just prequalified to buy your home, but that they are actually preapproved. A real preapproval means that the buyer's loan package has been submitted to a lending institution and has been approved. The only things needed to complete this loan are a purchase agreement signed by buyer and seller, a preliminary title report, and an appraisal. (Be advised that some lenders may generate a preapproval letter when really a prequalification letter should have been written. You or your agent should be able to ask a few questions and verify the actual status of the buyer's application.)

Many lenders also perform "desktop underwriting." If the buyer's credit is good enough, and if it appears their income and debt ratios are strong, the lender can submit a loan application immediately by computer and then receive, almost immediately, an answer from an underwriter. Usually, it will come in the form of full loan approval up to a certain amount, subject to an appraisal of value on the property or with certain conditions that have to be met, such as verification of the information submitted. This is, of course, the best kind of information to receive from a buyer.

When you enter into a contract with a buyer there will likely be a deadline by which they must have full loan approval. If they do not obtain full loan approval by the contract deadline, the buyer may terminate the contract. If the buyer does not terminate the contract, they will be obligated to purchase the home or lose their earnest money deposit. This ensures that your interests are protected.

Another deadline to watch is the length of time for which the buyer's loan is locked. A short lock period and a long escrow can be a bad mix! Early in her career, Mary once had a 90-day escrow, but the loan lock was a bit shorter. Unhappily, though all contingencies had been removed a month before, at the end of the escrow the buyer's interest rate jumped up and the buyers no longer qualified for their loan! The house did not close escrow at all. Most escrows here close in about 30 days, though some go to 45 or 60. Just make sure that the loan lock timeframe is as long as the escrow period.

Creative Financing

Because of the astronomical cost of housing in San Jose and surrounding areas, many buyers are choosing non-conventional loans so they can get their foot in the door. It is now somewhat uncommon to see borrowers in Silicon Valley obtain a 30-year fixed loan for 80 percent of the value of the home and to pay points, though this used to be the gold standard! Many buyers borrow a commonly seen amount (80 percent) with a hybrid product, which is fixed for a certain number of years (three, five, seven, or ten), and then the loan becomes adjustable. Some borrow a conventional percentage but do it "interest only". A frequently seen combination is the 80-10-10: with a 10 percent down payment, 10 percent second loan and 80 percent first mortgage. This product enables borrowers to avoid PMI (Private Mortgage Insurance). Others buy with 100% financing. More and more, move-up buyers are getting credit lines on their current home as a down payment in addition to a regular first loan; then, after they complete the purchase, they sell their first home and pay off the credit line. For families with small children who are in overcrowded homes, this can be a better alternative then selling first, while still in the home.

Some ideas our borrowers like are the *NIV* or *no-doc* loan, also referred to as a *stated income* loan. With enough money down, usually 20 percent but sometimes only 10 percent, buyers can get one of these loans. NIV stands for "no income verification," and designates a loan where the lender feels secure enough with the size of the down payment that they don't concern themselves with verifying the income stated on the loan application. The lender may simply verify that the buyer is employed and that they actually have the resources necessary to cover the down payment and closing costs. A no-doc loan is a loan where the lender does not require documentation of either income or assets (assets in this case being the money to cover down payment and closing costs). Both of these loans will have a higher interest rate, as much as 1 to 2 percent higher than conforming loans. But when buyers can't secure normal financing, these are still good loans to go after.

Many Realtors® have also identified certain people who have money to invest, and who would like to earn somewhat more than the prevailing 30-year Treasury rate. For 1 or 2 percent above the current 30-year rate, they are often willing to finance a smaller mortgage themselves. Sometimes such loans have balloon payments, meaning that after a period of smaller payments (perhaps five years), the entire amount becomes due. For people who have had credit problems but can demonstrate they are making efforts to clean up their credit, a loan such as this will often get them to the point where they can get conventional refinancing long before a balloon payment becomes due. When a buyer has very little cash to put down, a private lender may take other collateral instead, such as cars or business equipment.

There are many types of creative financing. All of them carry more risk to the buyer than normal conventional financing, and most will cost more in terms of interest rates. But there is little risk to you as long as the buyer has been preapproved. When you are looking for the right buyer, knowing that they have secured financing, even if through unconventional means, will ensure that your sale will be successful. Sometimes it's the only way to make a deal work, and if so, you shouldn't be afraid to sell to someone who is using creative financing. Just make sure you ask a lot of questions and have your Realtor® at your side.

8. We're in Escrow, Now What?

In considering the many things Mary Pope-Handy did to further the closure on my property, I would have to rate her conscientious follow-through as outstanding. It was not an easy sale to bring to fruition due to the fact that there were several people involved on the buyer's side. It was a purchase made by the father of the interested party with two other Realtors® working on behalf of the buyers. This made for complications.

This was my first contact with Mary Pope-Handy and she served as my representative in this sale. I had the added problem of an unexpected broken ankle. This meant Mary had to fill in for me in many instances as I was pretty much bed ridden.

It turned out that I chose the right agent. She did an excellent job on my behalf. Mary was diligent right down to the end of the transaction. She so impressed me that I will use her for consequent property sales and or purchases without hesitation and I will recommend her to others needing a top notch Realtor®.

As a former school principal I am accustomed to evaluating performances and Mary went to the head of the class in this regard.

—Kathryn L. Merry

Once a potential buyer has decided that they are interested in purchasing your home, their agent will prepare the actual offer, called a *purchase offer* or a *contract to buy and sell property*. The offer will then be submitted to you and your agent to be evaluated. This is often done in person, particularly if it is not a multiple-offer situation. A personal meeting has the advantage of allowing you to size up the other agent, to ask any questions about the offer or the buyer and to get an immediate answer. If the buyer's agent has an overwhelming demeanor (pushy) and you are timid, or if there are a lot of offers to review, this may not be the best approach. Ask your agent for guidance. Some buyer's agents will simply fax the offer over to your agent without calling first. This is not a good sign of professionalism! The way you receive the offer may tell you a lot about how the escrow period will go. In addition to a signed agency disclosure and the contract, the potential buyer will also present you with a prequalification or preapproval letter from their lender and a deposit, also called *earnest money,* to signify that they are serious about buying the home, that they intend to perform as promised under the offer and that they will come to closing with the balance of the money needed to close the purchase.

The initial deposit, or earnest money, is usually between 1 and 3 percent (though sometimes less). The reason for this is the Liquidated Damages clause in the contract. If the buyer and seller agree to Liquidated Damages, and the buyer later defaults (the buyer decides not to complete the purchase after all contingencies have been removed), the maximum amount of "damages" the seller can hope to keep is 3 percent. In some areas, agents expect the full 3 percent at the time the offer is presented. Others look for the 3 percent either upfront or in two installments, the second one being when contingencies are removed. Sometimes the buyer simply doesn't have 3 percent in liquid funds and it cannot be done, but generally, Realtors® will advise sellers to accept offers with deposits of 3 percent. (Anything above that 3 percent is really just "for show" since it is not really ever at risk for the buyer.)

Every few years we experience a very strong "seller's market" in which there is a severe shortage of available housing to purchase compared to the number of buyers trying to get into homes. This can be a tricky time for both buyers and sellers. Offers may be written with the full 3 percent deposit upfront, "as is," or with very short contingency time frames (days for inspecting the property, getting full loan approval and so on), or with the elimination of certain contingencies altogether. (This is not an all-inclusive list of strategies that buyer's agents may use in such a market. Some of these practices can actually be dangerous in terms of later setting yourself up for a lawsuit. So make sure that you have a very well qualified Realtor® assisting you!) If disclosures and inspections are available before offers are heard, buyers may have reviewed and approved them upfront and may submit the signed copies of some or all of them along with the agency, offer, copy of the check, and letter from their lender. A strong seller's market will make the process of reviewing offers a little different than in a normal market; ask your agent what to expect ahead of time.

As the seller, you have the final determination whether or not to accept an offer. In the best of worlds, you will find a buyer who has enough money, is highly qualified and is very interested in your home. But in reality, there are often good buyers who may be first-time homebuyers, who are getting a low–down payment or nothing-down loan, or are borrowing the earnest money to submit with the offer. We have submitted offers for first-time homebuyers with a promissory note as the earnest money. This is when the buyer promises to bring the money to closing, usually out of loan proceeds. We have also submitted offers with minimal earnest money; usually 1 percent of the purchase price is about the least acceptable deposit. It is then incumbent on your Realtor® to determine whether minimal earnest money should be a deterrent to the buyer's ability to purchase your home.

The buyer's agent may want to include one or more "extra" clauses in the offer to purchase to cover special requests. For example, they may want to have the carpet professionally steam cleaned prior to closing, and such a clause could be included in the contract. If the buyer is purchasing land on which to build a home, they would probably want to know if a survey, soil tests or other information is available. Again, a clause would be inserted to cover that need. There are so many clauses, and so many special requests by buyers, that to cover them all would be impossible. You, as the seller, can insert your own clauses as well, with the help of your Realtor®, of course. One of our most common clauses states that the seller has the right to rent back the property after the close of escrow. This clause might be important for sellers when they have not yet found a new home.

Assuming you are presented with just one offer (although during a hot market, multiple offers are not uncommon), there are three possible responses: (1) you can accept the offer as submitted and sign it, officially accepting the offer; (2) you can reject the offer and hope they come back with a higher one or that another buyer will come along; or (3) you can counter the offer.

Once you have accepted the offer without question, do not try to second-guess the process. It is not the time to worry if you accepted too little or gave up too much. If you've done your homework, and you got what you wanted in the deal, be happy. The buyer probably has an agent smart enough to advise them that the offer meets your needs and it was not worthwhile trying to squeeze more out of it.

It is absolutely silly, however, to refuse to respond to a legitimate offer. Hopefully your Realtor® will not let you ignore a good offer. Recently, one of Ken's Colorado sellers had a property on the market at $179,000 and an offer came in at $163,000. She reacted to the offer as

though it was insulting and would not even respond—
this from a woman who regularly made very low offers
on properties when she was the buyer. Ken told her that
ignoring the offer was not an option; she hired him to
sell her property and part of his responsibility was to communicate with every potential buyer until they either
bought the property or went away. She said, "Fine, then
tell them I'm holding out for full price." He did. Within
an hour, the same buyer submitted a new offer at
$176,000, and the seller accepted. There are, however,
agents who forget their objectivity, become emotionally
involved and take offers personally. When reviewing a
buyer's low offer, we've had listing agents tell us, with all
the resentment they can muster, "This is an insult. My
seller won't even respond to this." The agent should realize that they are not the seller, *you* are. If there is a viable
buyer who wants the property and is capable of buying
it, they will run the risk of losing a sale for you.

Finally, although most rejected first offers elicit a
counterproposal from the buyer you should beware.
Often the first offer is the best. The negotiating process
continues until you and the buyers have come to an
agreement on the price, terms, inclusions and exclusions
which work for both of you. If the agents and their clients have done their work responsibly, it should be a deal
that makes everyone satisfied, even happy. It will be a
win/win deal for everyone.

When you have agreed to all contents of the offer,
everything is signed immediately. It's not a deal until
everything is signed and the signature of acceptance is
conveyed to the other side. A contract is simply an agreement between two or more people (called *parties*) to do
certain things, and in exchange, some form of compensation is paid. In this case, when you and the buyer do
what you have agreed to do in the contract, the house
will be transferred to the buyer and you will get the
money.

So now that you have a fully ratified contract, you are "in escrow". Your agent should provide you with a timeline (it is good to provide it to the other agent as well, so that everyone is basing their expectations on the same timeline) so that you know what is going to happen, and when.

Some of Your Responsibilities Are:

- Providing the buyer with all necessary disclosures and reports. This will include your best representation of the condition of the property and anything affecting its value or desirability. (Ideally you'll have done this long before a buyer is even looking at your home so you can complete the forms without being rushed or under pressure.) Here are some of the disclosures and forms you're likely to provide if you are in a typical transaction:

    (1) Transfer Disclosure Statement (required by law in most cases),

    (2) PRDS Supplemental Seller's Checklist (commonly used),

    (3) Lead Paint Disclosure for pre-1978 housing,

    (4) Natural Hazard Report,

    (5) Environmental Hazard Report,

    (6) other disclosures as required by the contract or suggested by your Realtor®, such as the Megan's Law disclosure, an insurance claims history disclosure, the CLUE report and so forth,

    (7) any inspections you've had done on the property,

(8) a Preliminary Title Report, and

(9) if applicable, CC&Rs (Covenants, Codes and Restrictions), Association Bylaws and any required condominium documents such as association minutes, financial statements and reserves.

- letting the buyer and certain other people have access to the home for purposes of conducting any inspections, an appraisal, taking measurements and so forth (you may feel invaded the first two weeks or so, and it is often easier to leave your home when they are there measuring, inspecting, and so forth);

- answering the buyer's legitimate questions about the house;

- showing up at the appointed time to sign the documents to transfer title of the property to the buyer. This is usually done at a title company;

- maintaining the home in the same general condition as on the date of acceptance of the offer (keep watering and mowing the lawn, for example);

- providing your loan payoff information to the title company;

- providing access to your home for needed repairs;

- having repairs done prior to close of escrow (unless otherwise agreed to in writing);

- contacting utility companies to transfer services to the buyer on the day of closing;

- moving out on time and leaving the home in "broom clean" condition; and

- being available for the final walk-through to answer questions about the house and how its various systems, such as the sprinklers and furnace, work.

Some of the Buyer's Responsibilities Are:

- applying for a mortgage loan, if they haven't done this already, and providing all the information required by the lender to process that loan;

- getting the money necessary to close the purchase—down payment and closing costs;

- providing, and usually paying for, an appraisal to determine the current market value of the property (this is separate from the appraisal that you may have paid for yourself, earlier in the process, to determine the best selling price for your home);

- conducting any inspections of the property, usually with the help of a professional home inspector or other specialists (roofing, chimney, septic, pool, foundation, pest, soils, drainage, and so on);

- reviewing the disclosures and title and other documents provided by the title company and determining if they are acceptable;

- securing homeowner's insurance (it is advisable to do this right away);

- conducting a final walk-through of the house;

- deciding which lender and loan program they want prior to being in contract to purchase a home.

Buyers are advised *not* to switch loan programs or lenders in the middle of escrow as this could cause delays to the escrow and can be considered as buyer's default; and

• showing up at the appointed time to take title to the property and deliver a cashier's check or have money wired to the title company a day prior to the close of escrow.

Contingencies

Nearly every contract has contingencies which give one party or the other the right to cancel the contract if certain things about the property are deemed unsatisfactory, or certain obligations are not met. For the most part, the buyer has the ability to cancel the sale due to property and financing contingencies (if the property is found unacceptable due to disclosure or inspection information, or if for some reason the loan cannot be obtained as anticipated), whereas the seller really only has the right to cancel if the buyer does not perform their responsibilities on time. For example, the loan contingency clause requires the buyer to apply for a mortgage by a certain date and to get loan approval by another specific date. If the buyer's lender anticipates problems getting loan approval, it will be up to the buyers to cancel the contract by the loan approval deadline. In that event, the property will go back on the market. The buyer has the right to review the disclosures, the natural and environmental hazard reports, and the title and association documents, and if the buyer finds those documents unacceptable, they can cancel the contract and buy another property. Let's look at some of the major contingencies included in nearly every home purchase contract.

The buyer has the right and actually, the obligation, to conduct an inspection of your home to determine its condition and everything included in the sale. This contingency gives the buyer the right to ask you to remedy things that may reduce the value of the home, and to terminate the contract if you can't reach an agreement on payment for potential repairs. Depending on which purchase agreement is used, the sale can be for the most part, an "as-is" arrangement, or there can be a number of things that you guarantee in terms of the condition of the house at closing. So, as a seller, you may be required to provide a pest clearance, a leak-free roof, all systems in operating order, a chimney without structural damage, and so on. If you have conducted presale inspections, you will be prepared for most repairs that will be required of you. And if you have conducted pre-sale inspections, you may simply be able to exclude items for which you do not want to be responsible during contract negotiations.

Other contingencies can also be built into an offer, the inclusion of which will depend on a variety of circumstances. For example, perhaps the buyer must sell their current home before they will have the money to purchase your home. In this case, they will want a contingency stating that if they cannot sell their existing home, they can terminate your contract. If you are willing to accept such a contingency, you should use it as a bargaining tool—maybe in exchange for taking the home as is—and you should impose a definite time limit. You can also give the buyers a 72 hour right of refusal to buy the house without contingencies and then put the house back on the market to see if there are any better buyers out there.

During the property condition contingency period, the buyers can try to satisfy themselves as to anything affecting the value or desirability of the property, either physical or non-physical. This could include items that you may never have even considered, such as inspections for mold, the geographical orientation of the house or even how it may look to a Feng Shui practitioner. These types of concerns are increasingly common in Silicon Valley today.

If there are special problems with the property, the buyer may ask you to address them, and make their offer contingent on their successful resolution. For instance, if a neighbor has an outbuilding or driveway that encroaches on your property, they may ask you to take the necessary steps to eliminate the encroachment. Because you may already have an established relationship with your neighbors, it might be easy for you to accomplish, making the buyer happy at a very small cost. Often, conditions like this may not be discussed until the buyer has received and reviewed the title documents. While title documents address these issues in general, the buyer may want to amend the contract to specifically address those concerns they want resolved as a condition of going forward. Yet another special problem that you might want to keep in mind, having nothing to do with the property itself, has to do with times of a rapidly appreciating market. In this case, the buyer may request an appraisal contingency in the contract.

Inspection

If you are selling a condominium in a newer project, the buyer may feel comfortable conducting the home inspection themselves, but this would be inadvisable. The buyer and their Realtor® should review the condominium documents carefully, or hire someone with an expertise in reading these types of documents, to determine the responsibilities of the homeowners' association, to see whether their reserves are sufficient, and to check whether or not the package given to the buyer is complete. For example, if heat is included in the dues, the association is generally responsible for maintaining heating systems. It is also generally responsible for outside maintenance, including painting, roof replacement, maintenance of common facilities such as a pool or clubhouse and so on. But if the heating system is separate for each condominium and the individual homeowners are responsible, the buyer must also inspect the heating system. In that case, the buyer might need a professional. Even in new construction there can be problems and it is advisable to get a home inspection. Termites can arrive on the wood used to build the house and contractors may make mistakes in construction–the best time to find out if this is the case is before you move in!

A good home inspector has been trained in all the systems and details that make up a house. A good home inspection will take from a couple of hours to a full day, depending on the size and complexity of your house. Make sure the buyers know about important positive facts, such as a newly replaced roof, rather than letting an inspector guess that it is five or six years old. Inspectors are not perfect, and the reality is that their inspections are mostly based on visual perceptions.

At the completion of the inspection, the inspector may take the buyer through the home to emphasize what might need attention, and possibly educate the buyer as to how to maintain the home in good condition in the future. Those are things the buyer may want to discuss with you and your Realtor®. The buyer may ask you to remedy some or all of those items. Hopefully the buyer's agent will inform them not to "sweat the small stuff." For example, if all the buyer finds in the home inspection is a bathtub or two that need caulking, furnace filters that need changing, an outside door that needs a new weather seal or some other minor details, the buyer should agree to do the repairs themselves once they move in. However, occasionally the inspector will discover a condition that requires a specialist. For example, they may find a cracked foundation wall that could be due to something more than normal settling. In that case, they might recommend the buyer have a structural engineer inspect the foundation. Other serious issues, from the chimney to the furnace, may require different specialists.

It would be appropriate for the buyer to request that you correct any major problems, and in fact the contract may require it. If the heat exchanger on the furnace has a leak, it may have to be replaced, depending on your contract, which can be costly. If any appliances do not work, the buyer may ask that they be repaired or replaced. If the roof is in such disrepair or so old that replacement is imminent, the buyer may ask you to have it replaced prior to completing the sale.

When the buyer makes these requests, depending on whether they are contractually required of you or not, you can respond in a variety of ways. On the items for which you are not required to make repairs, you can agree to have the problems remedied prior to closing, if you think that the cost to you is reasonable in relation to the sales price; you can refuse on the grounds that the price the buyer negotiated on the house does not leave you enough money to make the corrections; or you may offer to settle with the buyer somewhere in between. If you have sold the home "as is" and do not have the cash to fix the furnace, for example, but recognize that it needs repairing, you can offer to compensate the buyer at closing and let the buyer have it repaired after the home is theirs. If you cannot resolve the issues, the buyer can cancel the offer and move on. In fact, if the buyer finds a serious, ongoing problem (like the foundation wall), the buyer may want to terminate the offer outright. Even if your home is selling in "as is" condition, the buyer still has the right to an inspection and can request repairs. You, as the seller, are not required to make the requested repairs, but the buyer can still cancel the deal on this basis.

Title Documents and Easements

The contract will describe certain documents that you are obligated to provide to the buyer, including a preliminary title report. Whatever form it takes, it is a legal picture of the title to the property. It shows who owns the property (hopefully, you), the existing mortgage company and the initial amount of your loan. Also, it shows other things about the property that need to be cleared up prior to closing or that might impede the buyer's ability to purchase the home.

The buyer and their agent or attorney will review these documents to ensure there are no title problems that would prevent the buyer from getting clear title to the property. For example, if there are liens or obligations against the property which total more than the purchase price, the buyer should immediately inquire how those debts are going to be paid. Typically, buyers do not want to take title of a property that has obligations against it which cannot be cleared by the title company at closing. It might be that some of the obligations shown in the title documents have actually been paid, but the payments have not been recorded with the county clerk. A simple recording of the documents would clear those debts.

Some problems disclosed in a title search may be very simple to remedy. For example, if the title is shown to be held in the names of both a husband and wife as joint tenants, but one has died, a simple recording of the death certificate will remove that person from the title, enabling the surviving spouse to transfer title to the buyer.

There are also things on virtually every set of title documents that will remain with the property even after sale. Utility companies which have power, sewer, water and cable lines running to the property will generally have a continuing easement to go onto the land for purposes of repair, replacement or installation of utilities. This is limited to the areas designated on the *plat,* the surveyor's exact drawing of the homesite.

An easement is not an actual title to or ownership of property. It is simply a recorded agreement giving access to another person or entity for limited purposes. Local governments might have easements for a variety of reasons, such as access to power poles. Some states may require homeowners in certain communities to set aside extra land to dump snow off the roadway, or in beach communities to allow for public access to the waterfront. An easement may give a neighbor the right to cross your property to get to their own, or to share a driveway if they are otherwise unable to get reasonable access to their home. Or, the buyer may have an easement across a neighbor's land. Easements are very common and should not necessarily deter a buyer from purchasing your home. If they have an experienced Realtor®, they should already be informed of this fact.

Common Interest Communities

Until the 1960s, neighborhoods were established and communities grew without a lot of community planning. In older cities, you will often find that homes in the same neighborhood are very different from one another. You may find a ranch house next to a modern house, or a shack next to a mansion. In the mountains you often see an A-frame next to a large traditional-style house. Commercial, residential and industrial components can be randomly interspersed. Over time, governing authorities (town councils and county governments) have usually developed rules and regulations that give them the authority to approve what is built, to ensure some consistency exists in each neighborhood development and to designate how homes, stores and industrial development will be separated.

Restrictions on building or remodeling, imposed by both governments and developers, have flourished in the past 30 years, but for different reasons. Governments want to control growth and developers want to preserve values. Additionally, towns or cities want to preserve historic charm, so older homes may be allowed to expand but with restrictions as to the facade or design elements. These are issues in addition to any CC&Rs.

Therefore, depending on the neighborhood, the developer may have filed documents with the governing authority that establish certain guidelines. These are generally called the *covenants, conditions and restrictions* (CC&Rs) for a neighborhood. Often these documents incorporate a set of architectural guidelines, which may be more or less restrictive than local building codes.

If you are selling a condominium or townhouse, the documents are called the declaration and bylaws. Because this type of property is typically managed by a homeowners' association there will also be a set of rules and regulations. The association collects dues, the amount of which it adjusts from time to time, and will have a set of financial documents showing how well it has managed the condominium complex.

All of these documents should be provided to the buyer along with the title documents. If they are not, have your Realtor® determine if such documents exist, and if so, have them get copies for the buyer. It is important for the buyer to review them. The restrictions imposed by these documents may be perfectly acceptable to the buyer. For example, some neighborhood associations will not allow anyone to have junk cars parked in front of homes and will not allow the buyer to conduct auto repairs on the property. The restrictions are designed to ensure that only certain types of people would live in the neighborhood—those who like the restrictions. If the buyer happens to be a backyard mechanic, this type of neighborhood may not work.

Some associations restrict the size and number of household pets. (Actually, some cities do this as well. San Jose has a two dog and two cat restriction.) Some condominium associations insist that anything stored on a deck (like bicycles) not be visible from the street. These restrictions and requirements should be reviewed by the buyer during the title review period. For example, an RV owner would be unpleasantly surprised to find out after closing that the covenants prohibited RVs from being parked anywhere on the property. But because restrictions are to be expected when buying a condo or a house in a planned community, this should not affect the sale. Some PUDs even have restrictions on the color of curtains that show through the front windows of your home, or whether or not the garage door can remain open other than when you are backing out of or pulling into your garage.

If you are selling a condominium, townhouse or other property that requires the payment of dues and assessments, you must, by law, provide the buyer with a lot of documentation as part of your disclosure obligation. These include the Articles of Incorporation, current bylaws, CC&Rs, operating budget, a summary of the association reserves and other reserves information, a statement regarding any pending litigation and more. A very good form, commonly used to request these documents in much of our valley, is the PRDS Request for Homeowner Association Documents. If reserves are not substantial enough, homeowners could be faced with future special assessments. That is, every homeowner is asked to pay a set amount (sometimes amounting to thousands of dollars) to pay for a needed improvement to the whole complex. (Earthquake insurance assessments can be especially expensive.) If the buyer reviews the minutes or places a telephone call to a member of the association board of directors, they can also get information about what the association is planning.

These are all things that should be disclosed to the buyer in the title documents. The buyer will have an opportunity to review these documents, and it is important for the buyer to voice any objections before the stated deadline. If there is anything they cannot live with, they have the right to terminate the contract within a reasonable period of time (usually designated in the purchase contract).

The Appraisal

If the buyer is having part of the purchase financed with a mortgage loan, the loan will generally be contingent on a satisfactory appraisal of value. The buyer has the option of including an appraisal contingency if they are paying cash, but it will be required by their lender if they are financing. This appraisal is the same as the one you may have had done yourself prior to determining the sale price, except that it is paid for by the buyer.

Again, an appraisal is a process whereby a licensed professional examines your home, reviews similar properties that have been sold recently and gives an opinion of the fair-market value of your property. However, at this phase, the appraiser also looks at the contract in place between you and the buyer. If they determine the contract sets a price that is fairly close to the value established by looking at comparable sold properties, they will most likely establish a fair-market value at or close to your contract price.

If your contract price is substantially different, then the fair-market value may be either higher or lower. If the appraisal is higher than what you have agreed to sell the home for, you should not be too concerned, especially if you did your homework. More likely than not, you and your Realtor® negotiated a very good deal. If it comes in lower (even by $1), and you have allowed the buyer to make the appraisal a contingency in the contract, they have the right to terminate the contract. The contract can be kept intact, however, by one of three agreements: (1) They agree to pay a larger down payment (because their lender will only lend based on the appraised value); (2) you agree to lower the contract price; or (3) you and the buyers agree to settle someplace in between.

financing

In most states the buyer loses their earnest money deposit if they default on the contract, and additional penalties could be imposed. If they are financing the purchase, they will usually request a contingency for such a case. In other words, the buyer would be given a certain amount of time for the lender to approve their loan within certain established parameters. In some states, if the buyer does not have full loan approval at terms acceptable to them by the loan approval deadline, they must provide you with written notice to terminate the contract.

If the buyer is having difficulty getting the loan they want and a lender suggests another loan that will work, you and your agent or attorney may want to negotiate a limited extension of the contract. Whether you agree to cooperate will depend on how interested you are in continuing to work with the buyer. If the buyer does not terminate the contract under a loan contingency and subsequently fails to qualify for a loan and cannot continue with the purchase, they are considered in default.

It is critically important that you, your Realtor® (and your attorney, if one happens to be involved) be cognizant of all contract deadlines and who must perform what obligations by each deadline. Then you will be able to protect your rights under the contract, including your right to earnest money if the contract is wrongfully terminated.

9. Preparing for Uncle Sam

Mary is connected. She is almost "wireless." As an engineer, I don't want to have to technically train experts in their field on the systems they use to do their work. In my search for a home I was very specific in my requirements. The tool most Realtors® use to sort through houses for sale (the Multiple Listing Service) seems to confuse and confound many Realtors®, but not Mary! I've seen ¼-acre properties listed as 44 acres, two car garages listed as one car garages, incorrect school codes, and poor descriptions for great properties. From a buyer's perspective, she knows the territory and can spot the errors. From a seller's prospective, Mary knows the best way to present your home. She knows the process and systems and works them to her client's advantage.

—Anne G.

W hether you're self-employed, a wage earner or own your own business, you know that Uncle Sam, through the Internal Revenue Service, is your silent partner. It's no different when you sell your home. When you sell it for more than you paid, you create a taxable gain. However, just as you were able to take deductions on your tax return for the interest you paid while living in your home, Uncle Sam has created some wonderful tax benefits when you sell your home.

Please be aware we are *not* providing tax advice. As we said at the beginning of this book, we've tried, we really have tried to be as accurate as possible when it comes to what works and what doesn't in selling a home. In this section we will talk about how the tax laws work in your favor as a home seller. We have attempted to ensure that everything said here is accurate and relevant, but laws change, circumstances vary and there is always the possibility for error. Using the guidance offered here, along with your selection of a competent tax professional, whether a Certified Public Accountant or a tax attorney, you should feel confident in selling real estate and legally avoiding taxes on any gain you may have created. If your situation is complicated by any of a number of factors—if the property is classed as a business, farm, ranch or multi-unit residence—please consult a tax professional who specializes in that area.

Let's start with the first tax advantage: It used to be that if you sold your home and purchased another, all gain from the appreciation in the value of your old home could be transferred to your new one without owing current income or capital gains taxes, provided you rolled that gain over into a new home within 24 months of selling your old one. This was under IRS Code Section 1034, prior to the Taxpayer Relief Act (TRA) of 1997. Section 1034 also replaced IRS Code Section 121, which was designed for taxpayers who were over age 55 and allowed a $500,000 exclusion for married couples or a $250,000 exclusion for a single person on the sale of their principal residence. Now you no longer need to buy another house of equal or greater value to claim the exclusion.

You can take advantage of the new law over and over again (although not more than once every two years), but there are certain guidelines. First, the property must be your principal residence and not a second home or rental property. Second, it may be a detached house, a mobile home, a co-op apartment or a condominium, but you cannot have more than one principal residence at the same time. Third, you must have lived in the house for at least two of the last five years prior to the sale. There is even a benefit to a spouse who is not living in the house at the time of the sale; they can claim up to

$250,000 of tax-free profits, provided they too lived in the home for two of the last five years. This also applies to two co-owners who are not married, as long as they meet the occupancy rules.

Even if one spouse dies, these tax benefits are available. The surviving spouse, whether widow or widower, is allowed to claim the full $500,000 exclusion if the home is sold in the same year that the spouse died.

Section 1034 eliminates most of the record-keeping requirements if you know that your gain will be less than $250,000. By the way, the gain you are allowed to exclude is the lesser of your gain or $250,000. In other words, if your gain is $100,000 on the sale of your home, you do not get to take a $250,000 deduction. In the past, your escrow company had to file a Form 1099-S and report your taxable gain to the IRS. This is no longer required. However, if you take a loss on the sale of your home, you can't deduct that loss; remember, you had been getting an interest deduction.

Investment Property Relief

Tax deferral is also available when you sell a rental home or an apartment building if you follow the guidelines in IRS Code Section 1031. This is called a *1031 tax-deferred exchange,* and is a powerful way to create wealth through real estate. You can sell investment property and transfer all of the gain to another larger investment property and defer the taxes that would have been due on a straight sale.

Here's how it works: An investor/taxpayer can avoid the taxes on the sale of investment property and qualify for *exchange* treatment if the property was held as investment property, or for use in a trade or business, and was exchanged from property that was like that which was sold. This is called *like-kind.* However, prior to the sale of the old property the seller must enter into an exchange agreement with a *qualified intermediary*. This person or company structures the exchange transaction to meet all of the IRS Code requirements.

What Is a Qualified Intermediary?

A qualified intermediary is also known as a *facilitator* or *accommodator*. This is a person or company who holds the funds from your sale and structures the transaction to meet IRS requirements. Unfortunately, there are no federal or state laws that govern an accommodator. Anyone can claim to qualify; however, it cannot be anyone close to you, such as your accountant, attorney, banker, employee or family member. You must confirm that they are qualified, that they have the knowledge, experience and credentials to perform for you. Also, since they will hold your money, you want to be sure they don't take an extended trip to a country without an extradition treaty.

Ask the accommodator if they pay interest on your funds. Ask for their fee structure and whether there are extra charges if you require additional consultations. Verify that they are members of the national organization for qualified intermediaries, the Federation of Exchange Accommodators (FEA). Confirm that they carry an independent bond issued by an insurance company that specializes in this type of coverage. This is one of the most important items. You don't want to be left empty-handed if your money is stolen by the intermediary or one of their employees.

IRS Guidelines

There are three basic guidelines set out by the IRS to qualify for exchange treatment. First, the purchase price of the replacement property must be equal to or greater than the property you sold.

Second, the debt on the replacement property, the mortgage, must be equal to or greater than the debt held on the property you sold. There should be no relief of your debt.

Third, all of the net proceeds, the total amount you received for your property, must be used to buy the replacement property.

If you don't follow these three guidelines, you can still complete the exchange, but you may have taxes to pay. As an example, if you hold out $100,000 from the exchange (this is called *boot*), it will be taxed. When attempting a partial exchange it is crucial you get competent tax advice.

Like-Kind Property

Like-kind refers to the type of property involved in an exchange. According to the IRS this is "any property held for productive use in a trade or business or held for investment purposes." As an example, you can exchange an apartment building for a commercial building, or a rental single-family home for an apartment building or a shopping center. Even raw or vacant land and a leasehold for 30 years or more count under exchange rules.

The following property is not considered real estate, and therefore does not count as exchange property: money, stocks, bonds and notes. Also, limited partnerships and your primary residence do not qualify.

Time Frame

Most exchanges occur as delayed exchanges, and there are two key deadlines to keep in mind. The first is the 45-day period to identify the property you want to acquire after the close of escrow on your property. The second is the 180-day period by which you must close escrow on your replacement property. There are no exceptions or extensions.

You have two choices when it comes to identifying your replacement property. The first is the *three-property rule,* and the second is the *200 percent rule.* The three-property rule allows you to identify up to three properties that you want to acquire as an exchange. You may purchase one or all of the properties to complete your exchange as long as they follow the IRS guidelines described earlier. If you choose to purchase more than three properties, you must qualify under the 200 percent rule, which allows you to identify as many properties as you want as long as the total market value of all the identified properties is less than 200 percent of the value of the sold property. You will need to complete an *identification notice* for your qualified intermediary to comply with the IRS rules.

Most often, when sellers consider a tax-deferred exchange they are dealing with large amounts of money. Competent advice is suggested because the penalty for failure to follow the rules is substantial. Please consult qualified professionals.

Section II

Buying Your Next Home

Buying Your Next Home

It is sometimes difficult to balance selling your home while trying to buy a new home. The timing is often hard to gauge and your decision will often be affected by whether you are in a buyer's or seller's market. Should you wait until you have a contract before you start looking? And if you wait too long, could you face a period of "homelessness"? Don't panic. Like all other aspects of buying and selling real estate, planning is everything. There are a couple of viable approaches to this dilemma. Most importantly, make a backup plan for what you will do if things do not go as planned.

Right now, an increasingly popular way to "move up" is to take an equity line of credit on your current home, locate your move-up home and purchase it, and then sell your first home quickly. The upside is that you won't be homeless. The downside is that you will carry two homes for a while—and that's expensive! It also puts you in a position of needing to sell your first home quickly, which is not to your advantage. Most of the time, a better approach is to sell your first home leaving enough time in the contract (either in escrow or with a rent-back option) to locate the move-up property. With the second scenario, you may have to move twice if it's a tough buying market, but you won't have to carry two mortgages at once. Your choices should depend on your time frame and your budget.

In general, we recommend waiting to look for your new home until you are under contract with a buyer, for several reasons. First, if you find a new home before you sell your current one you could be faced with two mortgages, which few of us can really afford—not to mention that the burden could affect the financing of your new home. Although you can use the equity in one home to finance the other, many banks will charge you a higher rate and you will have to refinance as soon as your house is sold.

Second, if the idea of two mortgages is unrealistic for your financial situation, you could get panicked and unnecessarily sell below-market. In the end this could cost you much more than the price of interim housing. Although you could ask the seller of the home you have your heart set on to make the purchase contingent on the sale of your current home, most sellers are unwilling to do so, due to the high risk it carries. This contingency could be particularly difficult to get in a hot housing market. And if your house remains unoccupied, you could pay substantially higher insurance rates, sometimes as much as four times your old rate, because vacant homes have a much higher risk of vandalism and arson.

Another option is to rent your house until it sells, but houses with renters are generally harder to sell. Renters take worse care of a home, so it never "shows" as well, and buyers are reluctant to deal with the possibility of having to evict someone if the tenant refuses to leave after the sale. Additionally, your lease with them might put restrictions on showing your home. The harder it is to show your home, the less traffic you're going to receive and ultimately, the worse price you are likely to get.

It really is best to sell first and have a game plan if you don't find something right away. Although potential "double moves" are expensive, you can try to lease back your sold house for a short period of time, or put your belongings in storage and stay with friends or relatives. If you do lease your home back after you have sold it, keep in mind that 60 days is usually the limit. Beyond that, the buyer's lender will consider the home non-owner occupied and will charge a higher interest rate. And, of course, you can rent some form of short-term housing. Since your Realtor® knows your needs best, they can often be a very good source for finding affordable short-

119

term housing, especially if you have children or pets. Although these choices may seem daunting or expensive, if you plan ahead they may save you the anxiety of owning two homes.

Another rule of thumb to follow is to buy first when prices are heading up, and sell first when they are heading down. That way you are in the best position to get a good deal in the market. Like we've said before, planning is the key to making a smooth purchase or sale of property.

10. Play the Field and Lose the Game

Mary is extremely knowledgeable about real estate in the Silicon Valley. She found a home for my family in a neighborhood I wasn't even aware of, but that suited my family's needs perfectly.

—Kieran Sullivan

Now that you are under contract with a buyer, it's time to find your new home. Perhaps you've been looking already, checking out homes on the Internet or going to open houses. But although you know to use a Realtor® to sell your home, now that it's your turn to buy, do you plan on using a Realtor®?

If you are like many sellers, you may be anxious to find your new home, so you have been calling on ads or for-sale signs, going to open houses and talking to agents to whom you have been referred. But generally, you have avoided committing to one, usually on the basis that you don't want to be pressured—especially if you haven't yet sold your home. But why play the field? You've already found a great Realtor® to sell your home, and maybe they can help you buy a new one.

Naturally, if you had a good experience with your agent in the sale, you would want to consider the same person to help buy your new home. Not all Realtors® represent both buyers and sellers, but it's always a good place to start, especially if you are moving in the same area.

If you are working with one Realtor® who knows you won't hop around from one to the next, they will become as committed to you as you are to them. They will become "your" Realtor®, and they will be working for you. They will likely work to help you get qualified for financing, and when that "hot" property comes on the market, guess who they're going to call? Believe me, it won't be the person who happened to stop in for an hour last weekend, it will be the buyer to whom they are committed—it will be you. After all, you are giving them a substantial amount of business and they will want to bring to your attention any property they can find that fits your needs. If it's a great deal, all the better.

We've sold numerous properties where our buyer was the only person to see the house. We try to check new listings regularly, network with other agents, and also watch the newspaper classifieds for homes being sold by owners. Sometimes we see a property that is obviously underpriced, or perhaps "priced for a quick sale." It then becomes imperative to get our buyer into the property before anyone else sees it, because we know it will go fast. We're off with a quick call to the buyer to let them know, "We've got one." We can usually write an offer to purchase or a contract that same day. We know the timing of your sale and we know when you need to find that new home.

We don't get paid until we produce a sale. There is not a lot of loyalty in this business, and there are a lot of short-term thinkers—people who will unknowingly lose thousands of future dollars to save a thousand today. You will find that two-way loyalty pays off. The key is selecting the right agent.

But what if you are moving to a new area and need to find a home? Obviously, you need to find someone who can represent your interests as a buyer. Well, we have some suggestions. One good bet is to look for a Realtor® who holds the designation of a "buyer's agent." If your own personal agent can't represent you because you are looking in another area, your Realtor® should be able to recommend a top-notch professional in your target area. Your local Realtor® can interview a prospective agent there and they will know what to ask to find you the right match!

Usually when you enlist the services of a buyer's agent, you will be working with a Realtor® who will represent your interests as a sort of personal representative. This is known as an agency relationship.

Agency

When you work with a buyer's agent, you will often enter into a representation contract. A buyer-agency contract is a contract between the buyer (you) and the Realtor®, and it works two ways. First, the Realtor® becomes your agent and is obligated to represent your best interests. Second, the contract represents your commitment to the Realtor® and says that you will work exclusively with them. This agreement means that when you see a sign on a property, you will not call the listing agent yourself to negotiate a deal, nor will you go into a property that is for-sale-by-owner to do the same. Instead, you will call your agent and ask them to get you information on the property. You now have an agent; use them. The whole purpose of this exercise is to get you the best deal possible. If you have selected a good agent, you should recognize they have the experience and the skills necessary to represent you effectively. It takes a modicum of trust to see that play out, and now is when your Realtor® earns their commission.

There are a few items you should pay particular attention to in a buyer-agency contract. In some states, most are already part of the standard contract, but elsewhere, this may not be the case. Before you sign, at least discuss the following topics.

Confidentiality

If you are to be represented effectively, it is imperative that the agent keep confidential any information they learn about you. In particular, your financial situation, willingness to accept concessions and motivating factors for the purchase should not be revealed, except as a valid negotiating tool with your prior consent.

In addition, you have a right to be assured that confidential information remains confidential even after you have bought your home or after your contract with the agent has expired or been terminated in any way. If you make an offer on an in-house transaction (where the seller is also represented by the brokerage representing you), your information should remain just as confidential as when negotiating for a property listed by another firm.

Scope of Work

The contract will contain a description of what type of property your agent is instructed to seek for you. Make sure the description fits your needs. If you are looking specifically for a residence, make sure the language limits the search to that. Do not accept language that says "any property." If you are considering purchasing a home from a family member or friend, you may ask to have that property excluded from the contract; however, you may want to ask your agent what they would charge to handle that transaction for you. Pitfalls can still exist and in fact can be more serious and more heart-wrenching when dealing with someone close to you. Many close relationships have been damaged or ruined when friends and relatives have done business together. It's usually not because of a lack of good intentions, but when objectivity is lost, personal feelings get exaggerated and hurt and the process erodes. We've worked on numerous deals where family members and close friends were involved, and we have found that it becomes vitally important to ensure a win/win deal for everyone involved.

Many buyer agents typically write contracts for six months, which is a long time. Often we work with buyers of second homes, and the process involves communicating while they are in another city or state. We will coordinate property showings with their vacations to the area, and sometimes they buy properties we've recommended sight unseen. Even when working with locals, using a six-month representation period makes sense.

This long period can be scary. What if you decide you don't like your agent? What if your plans change? The simplest answer is to ask for a cancellation clause. Always include a clause that says that either party, the buyer or agent, may cancel the contract for any reason whatsoever by providing written notice to the other party. While they may ask for ten-day advance notice, people who are not compatible should not have to work together. If your Realtor® is willing to give you this "out" in your contract, you can bet they are confident in their ability to represent you effectively. Keep in mind that you are not able to cancel a contract for a property on which you are already negotiating, and every contract will have what is called a "holdover" clause that entitles your agent to a commission if, after your contract has terminated, you buy a property the agent showed you.

The entire contract should be designed to be fair to both parties. It is fair to be able to cancel a contract when two people cannot work together. It is not fair to have someone do a lot of work for you and then cancel. You should be able to determine in the first or second meeting with your Realtor® whether or not you are compatible. Don't spend several weeks or months together and then decide to go with someone else.

Again, the bottom line is that if you do the same research to find a buyer's agent as you did to find your seller's agent, you should have the right person to help you find your next home (again, refer to the credentials mentioned in Chapter 2). If you are moving in the same area and can rely on the relationship with your present Realtor®, you are in a great position, but a buyer's agent is still the next best thing.

11. Mortgage Rate Deals

Mary and I had corresponded via e-Mail for quite a while before my husband and I made the decision to sell our home in Los Gatos, California. I was impressed with her professional tone and the informative data that she provided without pressing her sales pitch. As soon as I met her in person, my instincts were validated. She came across as straightforward, genuine and very knowledgeable.

It didn't take us long to select Mary as our agent and we were not disappointed. She acted with complete integrity throughout the process. Mary helped us establish a realistic price, played up the strong points of our home in her advertising and really took pains to mitigate the obstacle of our home being close to a freeway. Consequently, the house was sold in just over a month at a price acceptably close to the listing price.

In addition, Mary facilitated all the necessary inspections and reports and provided many other services to help us move out of our house. (She even commandeered her husband to help dispose of some old paint cans from our garage!) We were on a very tight schedule to close escrow and she maneuvered the process flawlessly.

From start to finish, I was consistently impressed with Mary's level of professionalism and service. I would not have any hesitation recommending her services to anyone.

—Judy and Ian Walker

Real estate is such a great investment! There is probably nowhere else where you can leverage so much with so little. You can purchase a $500,000 home with $15,000. If that home goes up in value $50,000 (or 10 percent) in a year, you've more than tripled your $15,000 investment (333 percent). Sound too good to be true? It's not. People do it every day. The best place to start investing in life is in your personal residence. If you are considering renting— don't do it! Renting is a losing proposition. All the money goes out and none comes back to you. As a homeowner, you get many benefits, including the tax advantage of deducting the interest portion of your payment. But for now let's talk about how to get the majority of the money to buy your next home.

First, you need to find a lender. Make sure you have a lender that specializes in providing loans for the type of purchase you are making. If you are buying a home, you will use a residential mortgage lender, and if you are buying land, with certain exceptions, you will probably use a bank. A mortgage lender can do land loans if you are buying a lot and plan to build a home on it immediately. Many mortgage companies now offer what is called a *one-time close, construction-to-perm* loan, which will help you finance the land purchase, provide the construction financing and then provide the permanent financing once the home is built.

Although we discussed lenders in regard to the sale of your home, once you are ready to buy it is your turn to find financing with the best terms possible. Whether you use a loan officer at a bank, a broker or a mortgage lender recommended by your Realtor®, you will want to make sure that they work hard to get you the best deal they can. At the end of the day, when you commit to a loan, the lender makes a commission. Make sure that they earn it!

In all states, banks are regulated by various government agencies in their practice of providing home loans.

In California, mortgage brokers are licensed, but mortgage bankers do not have to be licensed. However, in Ken's state of Colorado, mortgage lenders and mortgage brokers do not have to be licensed. This means anyone can get into the business, say they are a mortgage lender and do a lousy job, and you have no recourse through a licensing body. Even though many states require lenders to be licensed, lenders vary widely in honesty and integrity. Therefore, you still must be diligent in selecting your lender and loan officer; they can hold the key to your purchase. Be sure to ask your Realtor® about the licensing requirements for mortgage lenders, mortgage brokers and loan officers in your area.

A loan officer is much like a real estate agent: You may be referred to one by a friend, have a family member in the business or happen to meet one by accident. Just remember that not all loan officers are alike. A good Realtor® will have a short list of lenders and loan officers who have proven they know what they are doing, only make promises they can keep, don't spring last-minute surprises, have a substantial menu of loans to cover most situations and have competitive rates and costs. You want to avoid last-minute surprises like finding out a day or two before you are supposed to close that the underwriter has a list of conditions which will be impossible to meet prior to closing.

Beware of lenders who advertise low rates in major newspapers or on the Internet. Purchasers have often started their loan applications before they met and retained a quality Realtor® to assist in their home purchases. In many cases where the clients stayed with that lender, they have regretted their selection. Typically, something goes wrong. The most common problems are interest rate increases, disregarding good faith estimates, hidden fees, processing delays and lost documents. Make sure to get a lender who is both local and has been referred by someone trustworthy, such as your Realtor®.

We keep lists of lenders who meet our criteria, and a good Realtor® will also be familiar with the basics of loan processing and the types of loans available so they can provide guidance as you work with the lender and can tell if the person you are working with is knowledgeable. However, many agents simply refer you to a lender and stay completely out of the process. We feel teamwork will get more deals done and we tend to stay involved and brainstorm unique possibilities with our buyers and their lenders.

In a contrasting example, a recent first-time homebuyer, whom we'll call Bob, started out with a lender Mary had recommended. Then Bob found a "great" rate on the Internet and chose to go with the Internet lender instead.

Remember the earlier warning? Bob decided he wanted to switch his loan to the lender who quoted the lowest rates. Clients always have the right to choose their own lenders, but we do caution them when we are not familiar with a lender they choose. We cannot vouch for that lender's service, competence or knowledge. Often we interview a lender to determine the viability of the loan program they're offering and to get a sense of how well that lender can represent the client.

Because Bob found his lender on the Internet, the lender was from another state and therefore was not familiar with California's appraisal procedures. The lender was supposed to order the appraisal but never did, thinking that it was Bob's responsibility. Unfortunately this was not discovered until the day before closing. The closing had to be postponed and of course by this time Bob's rate lock had expired. Not only could Bob have lost the house, he also incurred the risk of owing penalties for defaulting on the purchase. But thanks to Mary's connections, she was able to get him a new loan through the original lender with a similar rate to the original loan's and in the end everyone was happy.

A good faith estimate is a form your lender provides you that shows the lender's regular charges, along with the other anticipated closing costs involved with the loan. It utilizes those figures to estimate the total amount of cash you will need to buy your house and calculates your approximate monthly payment. Some lenders will insist they cannot provide a good faith estimate until you have a property under contract or in escrow. That's just not true. Good faith estimates are simply that—estimates—and they can be prepared quickly and easily. In fact, some lenders we work with will prepare several, one for each loan scenario they are discussing with you. It assists you in comparing those loans so you can decide which one to take.

It also gives you something to compare with other lenders if you happen to be shopping for the best rates and costs. If one lender charges, for example, a $450 loan processing fee, and another charges $150, and the rates and other fees are the same, you might want to spend more time with the lender who charges less. But do not let these fees be the only reason for selecting a lender. Consider what happened to Bob. A good mortgage broker is worth their weight in gold. You should also get a good faith estimate on two other occasions: (1) when you have a property under contract, and your Realtor® provides a copy of that contract to the lender; and (2) when you change loan programs, either because you don't qualify for the one you started with, or you decide on a different plan. Once you are under contract, many of the items that were estimated on the first good faith estimate are known, so the estimate is more accurate and closer to reality.

Last-Minute Fees

Occasionally, one of our clients decides to use a lender we haven't recommended. In one case, a couple decided to work with a lender who was renting a home from one of their parents. The lender promised to cut his origination fee in half because of the relationship.

Usually, lenders charge a 1.0 percent loan origination fee. That fee is generally split between loan officers and the mortgage company they work for. In this case, the lender either gave up their portion of that fee, or worked it out with their boss to discount the deal. At any rate, when Ken compared his good faith estimate with other lenders, the reduced fee made the difference. Their loan was going to be about $140,000, so a 1.0 percent fee would have been $1,400. They saved $700 by going with this lender, all other things being equal.

Ken met with the lender and told him if he really took care of the clients, he would get other referrals from him. The lender was just getting established in the area, and he was eager for the new business. However, it took him longer to process the loan than he thought, and Ken did not have a settlement statement until the actual day of closing. Ken called him and the title company to bring something to their attention—the fact that there was a 1.0 percent loan origination fee on the statement rather than 0.5 percent—and asked for a correction. But this loan officer insisted he had met with the clients, and because they had not locked in their rates, and rates had gone up somewhat, he took a full origination fee rather than increase the rate.

Ken asked to see the new good faith estimate that he should have provided if this were true. He said he did not provide one, but the clients understood the new loan terms. The clients insisted there was no such agreement, and at the closing table they were faced with a dilemma. They had to close with the charges as they appeared, or get the lender to write them a check for the 0.5 percent difference or walk away and refuse to close on the home. They closed, and did not get a refund from the lender. They were angry with him but happy to be in their new home. That lender has never received a referral from Ken, and within a few months he was out of business, or at least gone from the area. He certainly does not rent from the clients' parents anymore.

Loan Types and Interest Rates

There are a variety of loan types available, and the loan program you select will depend first on your ability to qualify and then on your right to select one over another.

A starting place regarding your ability to qualify for a mortgage loan is the quality of your credit report. Every lender uses the FICO score, which stands for the company that created the scoring formula: Fair Isaac Company. It is a third party that provides the score to a potential lender. The lender does not calculate the score, but uses it to establish a borrower's credit worthiness. Until recently, the components of this scoring system were kept secret, but it's been announced that consumers will be able to get information about their score at www.myFICO.com. In general, they use different models and adjust the score depending on various factors, such as the amount of credit, the level of credit cards with no balances, cards with high balances, bankruptcy, payment patterns and so on.

At the current time, a score over 700 is excellent. Scores of 620 or above would normally allow you to qualify for A or A+ quality loans. These have the lowest interest rates and the most favorable terms. If we hypothetically use mortgage rates of 7 percent as the best available, a person with a score over 620 would qualify for that rate. Scores below 620 would normally put you in what is called a "sub-prime" category, also called "B" or "C" loans. The interest rate would depend on a variety of information specific to your credit report, but could be as high as 14 percent in today's market. The rules vary considerably between lenders on sub-prime loans.

In addition to the money the borrower would pay for doing a credit check, getting title insurance and paying escrow charges and appraisal fees, there is a cost to get most mortgage loans: *points.* Points refer to the cost of purchasing a loan. One point represents 1 percent of the loan balance. On a $400,000 loan this would be $4,000 to purchase the loan. If a credit score puts someone in the B or C range, the points could rise to 4, meaning it could cost up to $16,000 to purchase a loan. Other fees could rise from $275 to process the same paperwork for a typical A borrower to $650 for a B or C borrower.

Certain loans are specially targeted for first-time homebuyers and offer features such as low down payment (as little as nothing down), competitive interest rates and the ability to have a cosigner or receive down payment assistance from another source. There are so many loan variables that it would be impossible to discuss them all here.

At the time of this writing, second-home loans are available for 10 percent down with interest rates as low as on primary residences. Investment loans can be obtained for as little as 10 percent down (though 20 percent or more is most common), and the interest rates are somewhat higher.

The general rule is that the more risk you ask a mortgage company to assume, the tougher the rules will be. Government guaranteed loans (e.g., FHA, VA) take some of the burden off the lender, so they can keep the rules easier for you to meet. But conventional loans (anything not guaranteed by an agency of the federal government) tend to follow this formula: The more money you put down, and the better qualified you are to repay the loan, the more likely the mortgage company will be willing to give you good terms and rates.

Interest rates are around the lowest they have been in more than 20 years. The political and economic climate in this country have conspired to produce 30-year fixed rates that have hovered in the 6.0 percent to 7.5 percent range since 1998. It's at the point where nearly anyone with decent credit and a job can buy a home. You can't always get exactly what you want the first time, but owning, saving and taking advantage of a growing market may give you the ability to take your increased equity every couple of years and trade into a better home. And maybe you are someone who is doing just that.

Your Credit

As discussed above, in the past it was hard to be an informed consumer in the mortgage arena, because much of the personal credit information used by lenders was unavailable to you. You couldn't find out either your credit score or the criteria used to develop these scores. Consequently, consumers were unable to take proactive steps to improve their credit. Luckily, in the very recent past this has changed. The federal government has now passed a law that requires credit bureaus to release both your three-agency credit report score (FICO) and the bureaus' rating criteria upon requests from consumers. For a small fee you can now obtain this information, or as discussed previously you can contact www.myFICO.com.

There are also credit repair agencies that work with consumers to raise their FICO scores. These agencies work with credit companies regularly, so they understand how to fix mistakes and how consumers can rearrange or repair their own credit, possibly raising their scores as much as 40 to 100 points. This process can even be as quick as a few short weeks for people who need quick credit fixes.

There are also many federal agencies designed to help home buyers. They can help with home loans, credit counseling and even down-payment assistance. But beware of nonprofit credit counseling services. Although these services can consolidate debts for people who have trouble paying their bills, credit counseling is often looked at in the same light as bankruptcy when it comes to credit bureau scoring.

12. Loan Abuses

As a homeowner and part-time real estate investor since 1964 I have occasionally needed the services of a real estate agent. I can state, without reservation, that Mary Pope-Handy is far and away the most thoughtful, informed, thorough and helpful agent I have worked with. If we could clone the perfect Realtor®, Mary would be our model. I recently reminded her that her initials M.P.H. also stand for "making people happy." She has made *me* very happy time and time again.

—Karen Scarvie

Due to the fact that buyers often don't really know the exact amount of their loan or closing costs until they are at the closing table, there can be both the appearance and unfortunately the reality of loan abuse. Although this has changed somewhat in the last few years due to both truth in lending statements and the emergence of standardized closing costs, this is an area where you must make sure you protect yourself.

One reason for these recent changes is the current competitive market. A competitive market works to your advantage if you know how to make it work for you. First, regardless of your credit, in a competitive market it pays to shop around. Look for companies that offer a locked-in rate and standardized closing costs. This will avoid eleventh-hour changes.

You are also entitled by law to a truth-in-lending disclosure that should give you a fairly accurate reflection of your loan payments and the closing costs. Although these are never completely accurate, they are a helpful reflection of the loan and fees.

12. Loan Abuses

If your loan is for less than $333,700 (approximately), it is considered a conforming loan and therefore you can qualify for the best rates. The conforming loan rate is always going up, and even as we go to print it's expected to rise again in the next year. Check with your lender or bank to see what the limits are currently and if they are expected to rise soon. It could pay to wait a little while to take advantage of the new limit if you're on the cusp, since the difference between a conforming and jumbo loan could be as much as a 1/2 percent. If you are able to purchase a home with a *conforming*, rather than a *jumbo* loan, you will save a bit on interest. However, in Silicon Valley, with homes starting at around $600,000, this is not usually possible.

Another way you can protect yourself is by not just knowing who your lender is, but finding out ahead of time who will be servicing your loan. Servicing is frequently sold. Even though you pick a particular lender, after you sign the mortgage you may not have any control over the service. The "servicer" receives your payments, keeps records, gives late fees, follows up on delinquent payments and handles your complaints. Often the service you receive from these companies is less than desirable, since they have less invested in your business than the actual lender. But you can take some steps to control the level of service you receive.

If you have complaints about your servicer, you should send a written complaint, separate from your payment, to the lender's customer service department. If they do not respond within 20 business days (as they are required to under Section 6 of the Real Estate Settlement Procedures Act [RESPA]), file a complaint with HUD or the Consumer Protection Division of your state's attorney general's office. Don't just take abusive practices by servicers.

Also be aware of general predatory practices. For instance, it is now illegal for Realtors® and lenders to mark up the price of services that they don't provide, such as appraisals and credit reports. The best way to make sure you get what you are promised is to carefully review every document before signing it. You are the customer and mortgages are a competitive market. Be sure to demand the service you deserve.

13. Finding Your Next Home

Once you have established a relationship with your Realtor® and have your lender on board, you can look for a home with a much better perspective on what you can afford. Whether you are a first-time homebuyer, looking for a second home or building your real estate investment portfolio, knowledge brings understanding and control to the process. You will also be in a better position when making an offer because you are already preapproved for your loan.

The Search

Your search will probably take place in two ways. If you are web savvy and enjoy getting information directly, you may utilize a program from your agent, which enables you to receive, via email, MLS updates directly—several times a day! Mary's website offers this and more. Her website includes an "organizer" that also allows clients to save information on properties they are interested in and then watch to see if or when they sell, have a price reduction or go off the market. Many buyers enjoy the level of control these features allow. They can set the parameters for the search (areas, size of home, age of home, various amenities), and they appreciate the speed with which they get this information. Additionally, your Realtor® will be checking the Multiple Listing Service (MLS) to select homes for you to see. However, an agent is not limited to the MLS. They will probably be aware of new-home construction projects and might peruse the newspaper classifieds or otherwise be aware of homes being sold directly by owners. They will network with other agents as well to see what is available. Occasionally, they may have knowledge of a home or two that the owners have not absolutely decided to sell, but who are considering it. In addition, you might see open house signs or other signs on homes that appeal to you. A word of caution: Once you have selected a Realtor® and have an agreement to work together, if you see a sign on a house for sale, *do not* call on the sign. Call your Realtor® instead and ask them to do the research, let you know the details and set a showing if appropriate. Also, ask them how you should handle yourself in open houses. Keep in mind that the listing agent sitting at the open house or named on a front-lawn signpost usually represents the seller, and would like nothing more than to claim you as "their" buyer.

The homes selected by your Realtor® should generally encompass your stated parameters, including price range, number of bedrooms and baths, general size, garage and other physical attributes. They will be in your preferred neighborhoods, communities or school districts, and will have other characteristics you have indicated are important. As you look, you may find you cannot put all the things you want together in one package. You can get the home you want, but not in the right school district, and so on. You may have to refine your search several times. If you stick to the price parameters established between you, your lender and your Realtor®, then you may have to give up some of your preferences. If you are unwilling to give anything up, then you will have to take another look at financing—bringing in a family member to cosign, working with a partner or looking for properties in which the seller will carry all or part of the financing.

Even if you believe that the home you are purchasing is your dream home and that you will never leave it, listen to your Realtor®'s advice about which homes will have better resale value in the future. As we mentioned, many clients have traded up to better homes, often several times more than they ever imagined.

Recently, a past client approached Ken. When this couple bought their home, they swore they would live in it for 10 years or longer—this was exactly where they wanted to be. It was less than two years later, and they wanted him to list their home for sale. But they had second thoughts, because it would cost them an extra thousand dollars to sell. They reminded Ken that when they bought, he said, "I'll bet you a thousand dollars you will not be in this home five years from now. In fact, you will probably move on in less than three years." Ken forgot that bet, and of course they hadn't taken him up on it anyway, but it illustrates how people's needs and desires change over time.

You can also ask how much the sellers paid, why they are selling or about anything adverse in the neighborhood. You can't guarantee honest answers, but you will hopefully get a better understanding of whether or not this is the home you want to commit to. The bottom line is that if you have a plan, and you stick to the plan and understand your limits, you will hopefully stave off buyer's remorse.

There is no way to learn everything about a home before you buy it. You can learn a lot, and we will discuss some of those things here. But the neighborhood, your neighbors and future plans for the community are all factors you will discover over time. Your local government may decide to build a highway a few blocks away. Private enterprise may decide to put in a shopping center. Your job situation may change, or you may simply decide you would prefer living in another area for any of a variety of reasons. Very little in life is permanent. So while you may be perfectly happy with the home you choose to buy, do not be afraid to buy if everything is not perfect.

Insurance

Even if you never plan to move again, or you pay cash so there is no mortgage company making stipulations on your loan, you need to make sure the home is insurable.

Recently, a Realtor® friend reported receiving a termination notice from her insurance company. She had been insured with the same company for more than 25 years and had never filed a claim. However, the insurance company just found out that she lived more than 10 miles from a fire station.

Another Realtor® friend received a notice from one of his sellers who had recently listed a home for sale. The notice included a copy of a letter received from his insurance company. His insurance was being cancelled because his home was on the market for sale; the insurance company stated that having one's home for sale presented greater risk due to the fact that strangers will be going through it.

Any property you purchase that requires financing will also require hazard insurance, otherwise known as homeowner's insurance. Your lender will not provide financing without it. If you are purchasing a condominium, townhouse or other property that is considered a *common interest community,* this section may not apply. If the property has a homeowners' association that provides insurance on all the units, you will not have to purchase your own.

Insurance covers you for a number of things, the most disastrous of which being total loss of your home by fire or other calamity. Homeowner's insurance also provides you with liability coverage in the event that someone is injured on your property, and it covers you in the event of loss from theft or other smaller mishaps. Interestingly, however, some of the things that most dramatically affect homeowners are being decreased or eliminated from insurance coverage, such as coverage for mold and water leaks. As of this writing, we face a national insurance crisis.

The recurring theme of alarm in national, state and local meetings of Realtors® centers on the growing insurance crisis. More and more people are discovering that hazard insurance is hard to find or nonexistent. There are three primary reasons that insurance companies are refusing to underwrite insurance on new purchases:

1. The seller has either filed a claim, or simply called about a problem, and the insurance company no longer wishes to insure or reinsure the home. The current seller's insurance could refuse to renew or the refusal could come from a different company that has been contacted by the seller or buyer. The property may have had water problems, whether from leaky roofs, broken pipes or runoff, and the insurance company feels it may happen again or the property may have mold. The interesting thing is that the homeowner may not have even filed a claim. They may simply have called to see if a situation were covered and if they should file a claim. But overall, companies feel that properties that have experienced past claims are more likely to experience future claims. The property now becomes, for all practical purposes, uninsurable.

2. The buyer may have had claims on a prior residence that makes the buyer, in the eyes of insurance underwriters, uninsurable. It could be because of similar problems noted above. It could be because a company had to pay a claim because the buyer's previous home was poorly maintained. Overall, com-

panies state that buyers who have filed past claims are more likely to file future claims. Whatever the reason, the buyer becomes uninsurable.

3. The buyer may have low credit scores. What do low credit scores have to do with homeowner's insurance? Insurance companies have started to underwrite based on their assessment of a buyer's ability to properly maintain their home. In their estimation, people with low credit scores usually are unable to afford routine maintenance, leading the home to fall into disrepair and hence leading to claims-related damage.

Insurance companies claim a number of reasons for the current crisis. They point to the $40+ billion in losses in the World Trade Center terrorist attack and to major losses from natural disasters. They point to the surge of mold-related claims and call attention to aggressive low pricing in the past that resulted in major losses. What they do not point to, but studies have shown may be the actual reason for their loss of profits, are the losses they have suffered on their stock market investments.

The warning is clear: You can no longer take property insurance for granted. As of now, the traditional concept of automatic insurance is outdated! You must apply for and obtain homeowner's insurance at the earliest possible date in a transaction. Then, if denied by one company, there is at least time to shop for other coverage. You might also seek out an insurance broker who works with multiple lines. A broker would have a better idea of where to place an application based on either credit scores or claims history.

What is a C.L.U.E. Report?

A claims history report on a seller's residence called a C.L.U.E. report (Comprehensive Loss Underwriting Exchange) can be obtained from either of two sources. It is managed and maintained by ChoicePoint and contains information about claims filed on properties in the United States. About 90 percent of all insurers nationally participate in C.L.U.E.

C.L.U.E. reports are available on properties, not individuals, so when you make an offer on a property, consider having your Realtor® or attorney insert a clause requiring the seller to obtain a C.L.U.E. report. It will cost them approximately $13, and they can download the report from www.ChoiceTrust.com or request it by mail after downloading the form. If you find the home is determined to be uninsurable, it's much better to know in advance so you have time to work with the seller to check insurability with other companies. There are a few companies that do not participate in C.L.U.E., and a good insurance broker will most likely know them. Mortgage lenders require insurance, so if you are stuck with a property that is uninsurable, you would most likely have to be a cash buyer to purchase the home.

When you first contact a lender, immediately have them check your insurance scores to make sure you are not at risk of being unable to obtain insurance. And once an offer becomes a contract, make sure you apply for and obtain insurance immediately. If you have been denied coverage and received a letter from an insurance company, you can obtain a free copy of your C.L.U.E. report from www.ConsumerDisclosure.com. The report will show all claims filed in the past five years, including the nature and amount of each settlement. Examples could be water or fire damage or dog bites.

This issue of insurance has become so important that the National Association of REALTORS® has appointed an

Insurance Task Force to address the growing problem. The task force has already put forth recommendations for state associations to begin working on legislation, to educate their members and to discover other ways of handling the problem.

The Sale That Didn't Happen

One of Ken's earliest transactions involved Julie, a single mother who was selling her home and buying another. The home Julie was selling was called a "cluster home"—that is, it was located in a home project governed by a homeowners' association. It was just like a townhouse or condominium project, except the homes were detached. For Julie's soon-to-be-former home, another agent had produced a buyer and it was under contract. In addition, Ken found a home Julie wanted and put it under contract for her. Everything was going smoothly, except the lender for the buyer of Julie's former home did not get loan approval on time. Ken spoke with the lender every day and was assured the loan would be approved, even though this particular purchase was the maximum the buyer could handle. Their credit was fine and the ratios were close but acceptable, but the underwriter was overloaded, so they waited. Julie and her kids packed and scheduled a moving company.

On the day they were supposed to close on both the sale of Julie's old home and the purchase of her new home, with the house full of packed boxes and the moving van parked outside, Ken got a call from the lender. The buyer's loan had been denied. The lender hadn't noticed that there were homeowners' association dues involved with Julie's home, and didn't include that information in the loan package. Of course, he blamed Ken for not informing him of that fact, even though the information had been detailed in the contract, one of the first loan documents provided to the lender. Ken simply referred him back to that contract.

The situation was a disaster. The number of people negatively affected was enough to cause a relatively new real estate agent to quit the business before any more parties were hurt. The buyers' lease had ended and they had to move out of their apartment, now with no place to go. Julie and her two children had to stay in their old home and live out of boxes until Ken could sell it again. The sellers of the home Julie was scheduled to buy wanted to keep her earnest money because they were so angry, but Ken had the sale of Julie's home as a contingency in the contract and she got her money back. When Julie's purchase fell through, those sellers had to cancel their pending purchase of another new home. And, although less important to all of the frustrated home purchasers and sellers involved, none of the real estate agents involved in any of the transactions got paid. They all had to do their work over again.

Ken kept telling Julie through her tears that things happen for a reason, and they would get her house sold and find her an even better home to move into—which actually happened. When all was said and done, she had a far superior house to the one she would have bought, in a nicer neighborhood, closer to the schools her children would attend and she ended up happy. But what a process getting there! We wouldn't wish that on anyone.

Therefore, we build contingencies into contracts, and we try to cover all the bases so everything that is promised actually occurs. For example, every contract should have a clause that lets you go into the home one or two days prior to closing to do a final walk-through. This lets you verify that the home is in at least as good condition as it was when you put it under contract, and that the sellers have done what they promised. For example, if your contract called for the carpets to be professionally steam cleaned (note the language—you generally don't want to

147

settle for the sellers renting a do-it-yourself cleaner), you can make sure that was done. If certain things were to be repaired or replaced as a result of the inspection agreement, you can verify that they were.

It is common courtesy to have the house clean before vacating, but if that's important to you, put it in the contract. You see, contracts simply keep everything nice and tidy. If everyone you dealt with were completely honest, had an impeccable memory and always had it in their heart to do the right thing, contracts probably wouldn't be necessary. But even honest people have short memories, or get in a hurry, or decide they've already given too much, which makes contracts a valuable necessity.

Bring your Realtor® with you on your walk-through. Request copies of the receipts for all work done ahead of time, both to see that it was done and to have recourse with the service provider later if it wasn't done correctly. Sometimes, trades people will claim that something has been fixed, such as a reverse polarity issue, only to have you find out later that it wasn't fixed at all. Receipts help. Bring to the listing agent's attention anything that wasn't completed according to the contract, and have it corrected prior to closing. Practically speaking, rarely will something suddenly go wrong when everything is in place to close. You've probably packed or otherwise made plans to move out of your current residence, you are excited about being in a new home and the pressure is on everyone to go ahead and sign. So again, don't sweat the small stuff.

Anything significant should be handled with a written agreement at closing, or by setting aside additional money in escrow. For example, let's say the seller was to replace the furnace but couldn't arrange for a repairperson in time. You could all agree to have the title company or escrow company withhold that money from the proceeds due to be paid to the seller. The title or escrow company would then pay the repairperson when the work was complete. Or if the carpet was supposed to be cleaned but wasn't, the seller could hand you a check at closing to pay for it. Typically, if there is a holdback in escrow, we hold 150 percent (or even 200 percent) of the anticipated cost in case the job grows while it's being handled.

What do you do if the seller refuses? You have to make a decision. Is it more important to close, or should you walk away? We're not telling you this because it happens often, but because it does happen occasionally, it's best to be prepared. Check your contract for the wording on seller defaults too–it may stipulate what your recourse is.

If your transaction is typical, everything will have been completed per agreement and you'll sign the closing papers, present your check and get the keys to the house. Everybody walks away with big grins on their faces, looking forward to the new lives they have created.

Now for the fun part—it's time to move in to your new home!

To Reach Mary Pope-Handy:
Intero Real Estate Services
518 N. Santa Cruz Ave.
Los Gatos, CA, 95030
Phone: (877) 397-5391
www.PopeHandy.com
www.MaryPope-Handy.com
Mary@PopeHandy.com

To Reach Ken Deshaies:
Mail: P.O. Box 37
330 Dillion Ridge Road, Suite 6
Dillon, CO 80435
Phone: (888) 221-7669 or (970) 262-7669
Fax: (866) 782-6059
www.SnowHome.com
www.BuyerAgency.net
Ken@SnowHome.com

Visit our publisher at:
www.GabrielBooks.com

APPENDIX A

Moving Checklist

8 Weeks Before Moving:

❑ Create a "move file" to keep track of estimates, receipts and other important information.

❑ Check with the IRS to see what expenses can be deducted on your next tax return.

❑ Start pulling together medical and dental records and ask your health care providers for referrals in your new city.

❑ Start researching your new community. The Internet is a great resource for finding chambers of commerce and community guides.

❑ Get estimates from several moving companies and compare them.

❑ Arrange to have school records transferred to your children's new school.

6 Weeks Before Moving:

❑ Make a list of things that are valuable or difficult to replace. Plan on shipping these by certified mail or carrying them with you.

❑ Start working your way through each room taking inventory and planning what to get rid of. Start planning a yard sale and find local charities.

❑ Choose a moving company and reserve the date of your move.

❑ Start collecting boxes and other packing supplies.

❑ Check how to obtain new driver's licenses and license plates.

4 Weeks Before Moving:

- ❏ Send out change of address cards to post office, friends, subscriptions and credit cards.
- ❏ Hold your garage sale. Donate left over items to charity.
- ❏ Contact utility companies and notify them of disconnect dates. Arrange for utility service in your new home.
- ❏ Start packing items you don't use often.

2 Weeks Before Moving:

- ❏ Contact your bank and/or credit union to transfer or close accounts. Clear out safety deposit boxes.
- ❏ Confirm travel and moving arrangements.
- ❏ Return library books or anything borrowed from friends or neighbors.

1 Week Before Moving:

- ❏ Finish packing! Separate essential items that you will be taking with you.
- ❏ Empty, defrost and clean your refrigerator at least 24 hours prior to moving day.
- ❏ Cancel deliveries and services such as newspapers and trash collection.
- ❏ Drain oil and gasoline from power equipment.

Moving Day:

- ❏ Before the movers leave, check every room, closet and cabinet one last time.

❏ Upon arriving, inspect everything and make sure nothing was damaged during the move.

❏ Keep all moving receipts and documentation in your file.

After the Move:

❏ If needed, childproof your new home.

❏ Test security and smoke alarms.

❏ Set up all appliances.

❏ Get local emergency numbers and post them.

❏ Change the locks on all doors.

❏ Explore your new neighborhood!

Notes

Notes

Order Form

Regarding the REALTOR titles, we have many different state editions for homebuyers across the country. Even though they may be location-specific due to different state laws, the concepts hold true in any area. All of the buyer agency books are priced at **$17.95 each**. If you are looking to buy a home, please see our current state editions at our web site: www.BuyerAgency.net

To sell your home for the best possible price, buy a copy of:

Get the Best Deal When Selling Your Home, Denver, Colorado Edition,
   by Debbie Moore and Ken Deshaies $18.95
Get the Best Deal When Selling Your Home, Rockland County/Lower Hudson Valley Region, New York Edition,
   by Sheryl Vogel and Ken Deshaies $18.95

To order any of our books you can write to us directly, contact your local bookstore, FAX, or order online at: www.GabrielBooks.com

For additional information, please call (800) 940-2622.

Additional Books for Financial and Business Growth:

Couples and Money, by Victoria Collins, PhD $13.95
A vital guide for couples to thrive financially and emotionally. It provides exercises and instructions for couples to talk about money. Recommended by Consumer Credit Counseling Service.
Wealth on Any Income, by Rennie Gabriel,
   CLU, CFP (UCLA Instructor) $17.95
Move from creating financial goals to achieving them. Covers both the emotional and practical aspects of handling money effectively. Endorsed by Mark Victor Hansen, co-author of the *Chicken Soup for the Soul* series.
Wealth on Any Income cassette tape program $59.00
Five hours read by Rennie Gabriel from his book. It is a comprehensive but simple to use program for anyone to handle money effectively, get out of debt, live within their income, start investing with as little as $100 and ultimately create financial independence. Includes full book and two spending registers.
Money Talk, by Todd Rainey $17.95
A gay and lesbian guide to financial success including partnership agreements and health care powers.
How to Outwit and Outsell Your Competition, by Shirley Lee $14.95
Grow your business 50–200% per year using little-known, powerful strategies that cannot fail. Avoid costly marketing blunders by learning the common mistakes.

Order FormPlease Copy, Fill Out, Mail, Fax, Phone or Go Online

Name_____

Address_____

City, State, Zip_____

Daytime Phone (_____)_____

Email Address_____

Product Description	Quantity	Total
_____	_____	$_____
_____	_____	$_____
_____	_____	$_____
_____	_____	$_____
Sales tax 8% (only for orders delivered in CA)		$_____
Shipping and handling, $4 per book or tape		$_____
	Total:	$_____

❏ check enclosed $_____

❏ please charge my M/C or Visa #_____

Expiration date_____

Signature as on card_____

Mail to: Gabriel Publications
14340 Addison Street #101
Sherman Oaks, CA 91423-1832
or fax to (818) 990-8631
www.GabrielBooks.com